C000128563

Politics, Participation and Power
Power

Civil Society and Public Policy in Ireland

EDITED BY
DEIRIC Ó BROIN AND MARY P. MURPHY

GLASNEVIN
PUBLISHING

First published in 2013 by

Glasnevin Publishing, 2nd Floor,
13 Upper Baggot Street, Dublin 4, Ireland
www.glasnevinpublishing.com

based in Dublin, UNESCO City of Literature

A CIP catalogue record for this book is available from the British Library

Papers used by Glasnevin Publishing are from well managed forests and other responsible sources.

ISBN: 978-1-9086891-9-1

Contents

LIST OF FIGURES

ACKNOWLEDGEMENTS

This book is the result of our discussions and contacts with many people at various places over the course of the past two years. The editors would like to thank the members of the Board of Directors and Management Committee of NorDubCo, Dublin City University, the Department of Sociology in NUI Maynooth and the School of Spatial Planning in the Dublin Institute of Technology for their support, advice and intellectual stimulation.

Deiric Ó Broin would also like to thank the students (past and present) of the MA (Development) and MA (International Relations) in the School of Law and Government in DCU, and BSc (Spatial Planning), MSc (Sustainable Development) and MSc (Local Development and Innovation) in the School of Spatial Planning, DIT, for their willingness to engage with so many of the ideas contained in the book. A special debt of gratitude to the women in my life, my late mother who encouraged me to continue my education, Kathleen who put up with many late night proofing and editing sessions and Sarah who, in her own unassuming way, persuaded me to complete the project so she could watch Elmo on the laptop.

Mary P. Murphy would like to thank NUIM public policy students who attended the series of lectures. Thanks also for the inspiration of colleagues and everyone who continues to fight for equality and who, despite the odds, find many ways to enhance participation in public policy. Special thanks to the seminar participants from local communities, partnerships and local councils in North Dublin. As always thanks to Emer, Dan and all the family, your support is acknowledged and appreciated

We would both like to acknowledge the contributions made by colleagues in the North Dublin Political Economy Discussion Group. These were often challenging but always helpful.

Finally we would like to thank Dr. Helen McGrath of Glasnevin Publishing for her patience and guidance. There would not be a book without it.

CONTRIBUTORS

Mike Allen is Director of Advocacy, Development, Communications and Research at the homeless and housing charity Focus Ireland. He is also a member of the Steering Committee of The Advocacy Initiative, a collaboration of community and voluntary organisations with the aim of promoting the role of social justice advocacy work. He is a member of the Co-ordinating Committee of Claiming our Future. He was former General Secretary of the Labour Party (2000 – 2008) and of the Irish National Organisation of the Unemployed (1987 – 2000).

Matthias Borsheid is the Local Development and Education Manager of Northside Partnership, a local development company based in Dublin. Previously, he has worked in Germany in the field of research, economic development and the management of a regional European Union-funded LEADER+ Initiative. He is a member of the Irish Local Development Network's (ILDN) Research and Evaluation Committee and has been involved in the Centre for Effective Services' (CES) Specialist Group, which has been focusing on exploring evidence-based practices in community development work. He is currently a director on the board of a number of Dublin-based community organisations.

Paul Ginnell has been the Policy Officer with EAPN Ireland since 2005. Paul's role is to support people experiencing poverty and social exclusion and their organisations, many of which are members of EAPN Ireland, to understand and to contribute to policy making in Ireland and the EU. This involves regular engagement with members and policy makers. He also represents EAPN Ireland on the EU Inclusion Strategies Working Group which was established by EAPN (Europe) and previously on the Structural Funds Working Group. Before coming to EAPN Ireland Paul was Coordinator of an EQUAL Community initiative in Co. Westmeath and has also worked with the Limerick Travellers Development Group and the Irish Traveller Movement. Paul is a qualified Community Worker and also has a Masters in Applied Social Studies

Chris McInerny is a lecturer in the Department of Politics of Public Administration in the University of Limerick. His primary research interests focus on the interactions between the concepts, practices and processes of governance and social inclusion / exclusion, participatory democracy, the role of civil society in social change and the role of public administration in promoting social justice and social equity. He has published chapters and reports on governance, local and community development and has previously worked in a variety of civil society and international organisations.

Gary Murphy is Associate Professor of Government in the School of Law and Government in the Dublin City University. He is a former editor of Irish Political Studies, the leading journal of political science in Ireland published by Taylor and Francis. In 2007 he was appointed DCU's first Dean of Graduate Studies and served in that position until 2011. He was President of the Political Studies Association of Ireland from 2009 to 2012. In 2011-12 he was visiting Fulbright Professor of Politics in the Center for European Studies at the University of North Carolina, Chapel Hill. He is currently the Head of the School of Law and Government.

Mary P. Murphy is a lecturer in Irish Politics and Society in the Department of Sociology, National University of Ireland Maynooth. She primarily works in the field of political sociology and has interests in gender and social security, globalisation and welfare states, the politics of redistribution and power and civil society. She has published widely, most recently, *Careless to Careful Activation: Making Activation Work for Women* (Dublin NWCI 2012) and *Towards the Second Republic: Irish Politics after the Celtic Tiger* (with Peadar Kirby, Pluto Ireland, 2011). Prior to academic life she worked full time in social justice campaigning groups including Claiming Our Future. She continues to be an active public advocate for social justice and gender equality and is a member of the Irish National Advisory Group on Taxation and Social Welfare

Padraig Murphy is a lecturer in Communications at Dublin City University. He is currently the Programme Chair of the MSc in Science Communication and Director of the Celsius Research Group at DCU. His research work looks at communicative processes that interact between experts and non-experts and public engagement with emerging technologies. He particularly researches communities of interest and concern that build in acceptance or resistance of those emerging technologies that create public and political controversy, for example nanotechnology, embryonic stem cell therapies and genetically modified food. He is on the Management Board of the Community Knowledge Exchange at DCU.

Emma O'Brien is an education professional, with over 12 years experience in the development and delivery of education training initiatives in a variety of fields. She has particular interest in the development of new methodologies for communicating and promoting health issues. Throughout her career, Emma has gained research expertise in the fields of science & health communication, science education, e-health and entrepreneurial training. She is currently the Education, Outreach and Entrepreneurship Manager at the Biomedical Diagnostics Institute (BDI) where she is responsible for delivering the Institute's education, training and public outreach programme. Emma and her team have developed a comprehensive, innovative biomedical education programme, which is far reaching and enables the BDI to interact with students of all ages and the general public. The Biomedical Diagnostics Institute (BDI) hosted at Dublin City University is a Science Foundation Ireland funded Centre for Science, Engineering and Technology (CSET).

Deiric Ó Broin is Director of NorDubCo, North Dublin's regional think tank, in DCU. Prior to coming to DCU he was employed as an economic policy analyst in the private sector. From 1995-1997 he worked in the Office of Labour Affairs in the Department of Enterprise, Trade and Employment, and in the Office of the Tánaiste as a public policy adviser. His teaching and research interests include innovation and local governance, public participation and public policy. He was Convenor of the PSAI's Urban Policy Specialist Group from 2007-2011 and is currently the Deputy Convenor of the PSAI's Local Government Specialist Group and a member of the Regional Studies Association (Irish Branch) Executive Committee.

Helena Sheehan is professor emeritus at Dublin City University. She is author of books such as *Marxism and the Philosophy of Science: A Critical History*, *Irish Television Drama: A Society and Its Stories* and *The Continuing Story of Irish Television Drama: Tracking the Tiger*, as well as numerous articles, chapters and conference papers on philosophy, politics, history, media and culture. She has also been active in social and political movements since the 1960.

CHAPTER 1
INTRODUCTION

Deiric Ó Broin and Mary P. Murphy

Introduction

The book can be seen as a sister volume to *Power, Dissent and Democracy: Civil Society and the State in Ireland* published in 2009 which critically assessed the nature of the state-civil society relationship as it had evolved and offered perspectives on how it might continue to change in the near future. A feature of this book, and those that preceded it, is our desire to combine academic knowledge with the experience of those involved in public policy formulation at a variety of levels and in different roles. We are delighted that so many excellent contributors were able to make an input.

Focus of the debate

The crisis has caused the fitness of our representative political institutions to come under the microscope, but with some notable exceptions (e.g. Carney and Harris 2012), less attention has been paid to civil society's participation in public policy and its capacity to improve policy making. This volume brings together a number of perspectives on participation in policy making and critically examines the participation of civil society and public policy formulation in Ireland.

A number of concerns motivated this publication. As McInerney observes while the theory of participation has become popularised the actual space in the public sphere for participation has actually narrowed. A demand for a more participative and deliberative democracy brings into focus the types of governance arrangements required for a complex networked society of more critical citizen. Deliberative politics focuses political decision making as 'talk-centric' rather than vote-centric. Participation can be differentiated from deliberation, the OECD (2003) identified three general themes relating to citizen engagement in policy making: information, consultation and participation. At its most inclusive level participation means citizens engaging in defining issues, having a role in structuring the consultation process and having clear end impact on policy outcomes.

A key feature of the last two decades was the emergence of networked governance and various forms of participative processes that offered the possibility of power sharing. Some of these were initiated by the state and others by society, some worked, others did not. It is not always clear what were the motivations for enabling 'public' participation in policy making, it is not always clear who the public is and how that public constructed, in one way we can discern a move to associational democracy and participation of sectoral groups, in another way we can see shifts away from groups to engagement with individual citizens.

Central to these developments is the idea that decisions are legitimated by the degree to which the people impacted by them have the right and opportunity to "participate in deliberation about their content, and as a result grant their reflective assent to the outcome" (Dryzek 2007: 242). To what degree is a focus on participation a legitimation strategy? To what degree is it motivated by a desire to improve policy outcomes or public acceptance of public outcomes? Can we differentiate these two objectives?

Different discourses of 'public' are evident (Barnes, Newman and Sullivan 2007: 9) and it is not always clear what underlying ideology is driving any shift to participation, we see 'empowered' public participation discourses where participation is assumed to enable and empower disadvantaged groups, we see 'consumer publics' encouraged to participate in customer feedback processes with the state, we see 'stakeholder publics' where all are assumed to have a vested interest in or a stake in being part of the process, we also see discourses about a 'responsible public ' where a public who participate in a policy making process are assumed and expected to have a responsibility in delivering its implementation. Contributors to this edition considered their experience of specific models of participation and specific mechanisms used to facilitate public participation. They were asked to reflect on institutional barriers to public participation. We were curious about instances of direct input into public policy that changed policy or impacted on implementation of policy and how these differed across the sectoral experiences of public participation in public policy.

Of course many argue the process is as important as the outcome so we are interested in evaluation of the participation processes discussed in the volume and what issues arise with regard to the expectations of the public. Has participation enabled active citizenship or an active society? Has it contributed towards educating public and enabling society to be more inter-dependant? Do processes of participation create demands for more participation and consultation? How are these demands managed and translate into 'public policy' processes concerning public participation in policy making?

The first chapter by Chris McInerney is a rich discussion of key issues and trends in participatory democracy. The chapters are then grouped into four sub themes relating to partnership, poverty, policy making and public sphere. Section one and the next two chapters focus on the key theme of participation in partnership and its institutionalisation as a particularly Irish form of participation in policy making. Gary Murphy's chapter on partnership reminds us that Irish society had not discovered partnership in 1987 but had long been open to a corporatist model of key sectors participating in power sharing on economic and social policy. Deiric Ó Broin's review of local partnership and participative structures reminds us that without local government's willingness to cede a policy making role to local citizens the transformative potential of new governance arrangements will remain unrealised.

Section two's chapters on poverty offer very different insights into the experience of participation and deliberation from the perspective of the poor. Matthias Borsheid's chapter shows that the transformative potential of Asset Based Community Development on outcomes remains unrealised. Paul Ginnell's chapter reflects on the well meaning but poorly executed effort of the European Union to devise a process of stakeholder consultation underpinned by a principle that the poor should have the right to participate in the process of decision making. Mike Allen's reflections on the experiences of the homeless sector and homeless people can be used to reflect on wider experiences of poor people and their representative organisations' participation in policy processes and wider public debate. Section three comprises two chapters on public policy formulation and the role participation can play in changing public values, public education and creative problem solving. Emma O'Brien's focus on the linkages between the public, science and the health diagnostics industry is interesting for the absence of the state as a stakeholder. Padraig Murphy's examination of citizens' juries as a method of involving the public with nanotechnology is a practical insight into the dogged challenges of

3

involving the public and the time and resources needed. Section four argues that participation cannot be separated from the public sphere and examines ways that people try to create and engage in debates about change. As examples of forms of engagement with power and participation Chapters Ten and Eleven contrast two new very different forms of engagement in the public sphere. Mary P. Murphy's case study of *Claiming Our Future* is an example of values-led deliberation and participation and is followed by a different perspective of power and participation in Helena Sheehan's review of the experience of the 2011 Dublin Occupy Movement. In Chapter Twelve Mary P Murphy and Deiric Ó Broin conclude by drawing out key lessons across the eleven chapters and take the opportunity to explore some further themes including issues of inequalities in participation, the potential of information technology in enabling participation and the role of protest, the most traditional and fundamental form of public participation in policy making. They conclude by observing the need to strengthen the public sphere to support a shift in orientation towards a more participatory form of citizenship aligned with a meaningfull reform of the institutions of representative democracy.

Background to NorDubCo Martin McEvoy Series

This book is the culmination of the Martin McEvoy Seminar Series run by NorDubCo in Dublin City University (DCU) in late 2010. The seminars were organised and led by Mary P. Murphy (NUIM) and Deiric Ó Broin (NorDubCo). NorDubCo is a coalition of public stakeholders established in 1996 to promote the economic, social and civic development of the North Dublin region. Its members currently include Dublin City University, Dublin City Council, Fingal County Council, Northside Partnership, Tolka Area Partnership, Fingal LEADER Partnership, Ballymun Whitehall Area Partnership and Blanchardstown Area Partnership. The motive force behind NorDubCo's establishment was the shared belief that local government, local development agencies, the local university, local civil society organizations and local communities working together could make a difference to the region.

At that time a very specific set of challenges faced the region and NorDubCo was configured to address those challenges. The recent period of prolonged economic growth and subsequent economic decline have changed many of the issues facing the region. In some cases, old issues are at least partially resolved or no longer as problematic. In others, changes in the economy have created a completely new set of issues to be addressed by the members of NorDubCo. Throughout this period, NorDubCo has worked to ensure that sustainable economic, social and civic development take place in the region. As part of this it has worked to create a positive vision for community and working life for the region, a vision that seeks to embrace all of the region's communities. In operationalising this vision, NorDubCo's work has a number of distinct objectives. Of particular relevance is its contention, reflecting that of our stakeholders, that the region needs to develop a more inclusive policy debate and promote new thinking to influence the economic, social and civic environment.

In working towards these objectives NorDubCo works with representatives from a wide variety of civil society organizations, the business community, local government, the local development sector, public representatives (both local and national), education establishments (secondary, further and higher), the media, and state and semi-state institutions. The development of these relationships allows NorDubCo to facilitate a broad range of policy discussions between various stakeholders. Underpinning these efforts is the shared belief that a fundamental challenge facing North Dublin is to overcome barriers to shared decision–making. This requires a climate conducive to *negotiated governance*, i.e. the involvement of variable networks of communities, civil society actors and other stakeholders in the relevant policy formulation and decision-making processes. Developing this form of governance involves addressing the issues of building and sustaining a social and civic environment facilitative and supportive of such a process, and developing an inclusive decision-making process that is responsive to both the long-term and immediate needs of communities, as well as the infrastructural and developmental requirements of enterprise in the region. It requires paying particular attention to inclusion and participation of the most disadvantaged.

As a contribution to the development of such a form of negotiated governance NorDubCo devised a Public Dialogue Programme in conjunction with our colleagues in Dublin City University. This programme of activities is based on an understanding that civic involvement is the foundation of a thriving, vibrant civil society and a recognition that a space for dialogue about issues of public importance is often lacking. It is our earnest hope that NorDubCo's Public Dialogue

Programme contributes to addressing of these issues. An important component of our programme is the annual Martin McEvoy Seminar Series. The seminar series commemorates the former chairperson of NorDubCo. Martin served as Chairperson of NorDubCo from 1999 until 2007 and his commitment was both unceasing and constructive. He always played a pivotal role in our work. Whether it was sailing, his beloved Suttonians, business or local development, he was professional, dedicated and committed. He served with the Tolka Area Partnership as chairperson for their first five years and in the process supported hundreds of local people in setting up businesses or finding worthwhile employment. Martin was a founding member and former President of the North Dublin Chamber of Commerce and in addition he was an active member of the Council of the Dublin Chamber of Commerce. He also chaired the Fingal Enterprise Board, again supporting scores of new businesses to get started and grow. He served as chairperson of two boards in Corduff and Ladyswell in West Dublin. One provided a support service to elderly residents in the area and the other oversaw the establishment of a local youth and sports facility. All of this was after he had officially retired. Martin represented everything that was positive about the business community in North Dublin. He believed it was his community of which he was an integral part and he should serve as best he could in helping it develop. In a very practical way he believed in the common good and worked for it in a variety of ways, often with thanks and recognition, often without.

As an organisation we were diminished by Martin's untimely death. We lost a great friend and colleague with his passing. He had time for everyone and treated everyone equally. He will be remembered fondly for the genuine person that he was and it was a privilege for those of us fortunate enough to work with him.

As a way of commemorating Martin, NorDubCo's board of directors decided to rename our annual seminar series in his memory. We feel it was appropriate because he was also intensely curious about ideas and thought the seminar series, and its audience of politicians, students, public servants and community activists engaged in debate and, more often than not, disagreement was a great addition to the region. As he often observed, over a coffee after a particularly intense debate, 'this type of discussion changes the way people see problems'. We hope to continue to do so for many years to come.

The Seminar Series has been running since 2001 and each year attempts to address issues of contemporary concern. As noted earlier, the aim is not just to present information but to develop a dialogue between presenter and audience and amongst the audience itself, in order to develop a fuller, more robust and shared understanding of the various issues under discussion. It was in this context that Mary P. Murphy and Deiric Ó Broin devised the parameters for the chapters in this volume. Two chapters were not part of the seminar series but we included them as we feel they add particular value. McInerney's provides a rich and contemporary theoretical overview and Sheehan's provides a very personal experience of being involved in a potential powerful participatory initiative. We regret that one contribution to the seminar series on business lobbying and public policy is not in this edition, the work is poorer for its absence

Mary P. Murphy and Deiric Ó Broin
24th July 2012

CHAPTER 2
PARTICIPATION IN PUBLIC POLICY

Chris McInerney

Introduction

In recent times, notions of participatory democracy, civic engagement, community involvement in public policy and other related ambitions have been subject to an increase of academic, state and civil society analysis and examination. A variety of reports produced by international organisations, including a multiplicity of UN agencies, the European Commission, the Council of Europe, the OECD as well as national governments and non-governmental agencies alike line up alongside equally numerous academic papers, articles and books to argue the merits and demerits of deeper citizen participation (Cornwall 2002; Cornwall 2004; Narayan *et al.* 2000). Influential international organisations, such as the OECD (2001: 19), have some time ago asserted that "There is a growing demand for transparency, accountability and participation" and, as a result, "new forms of representation and types of public participation are emerging in all OECD member countries (such as civil society organisations) and traditional forms are being renewed (e.g. public hearings) to give greater substance to the idea of government 'by the people'". Far from being an abstract and idealistic aspiration, therefore, the OECD suggests that there are distinct benefits to be gained from such increased participation, particularly: improved quality of policy making through new information, perspectives and solutions; enhanced transparency and accountability; strengthened public trust in government; potential that enhanced collaboration can outweigh conflict as well as a general contribution to good governance.

However, despite these endorsements, it is far from clear that public participation in policy making and/or implementation has become deeply embedded in the mindsets of the political and bureaucratic classes or indeed, in all elements of civil society. In Ireland in particular it would appear that the space for public participation in dialogue about key policy issues affecting the country's future has contracted sharply in recent times, not least due to the weak developments between public participation and democratic development.

Public participation and democratic development

Setting the notion of public participation in policy making in a democratic framework is an important first step, given the charges sometimes levelled that prominent participatory processes such as social partnership are fundamentally undemocratic, an argument represented in one populist newspaper by the banner headline "Rotten Social Partnership Deal Eroding Democracy" (Ruddock 2006).

Actual or desired participation by a range of different groups and individuals in the framing and design of public policy, many argue, is a democratic activity, some would say a democratic right. However, there is a long road to travel from the forthright views of Joseph Schumpeter's on restricted democratic participation before you arrive at the type of democratic nirvana espoused by advocates of deep or participatory democracy. In order to fully appreciate the complexities of participation in public policy, some familiarity with the landscape encountered on this journey is helpful.

At one end of the democratic spectrum, Schumpeter's views on elitist democracy are sometimes presented as the archetypal elitist position against which real world practice could be contrasted. In rejecting any broadening of the base of decision makers beyond those chosen in competitive elections, Schumpeter argued that agencies that operate with a minimum of direct democratic control may actually produce decisions that are more readily accepted by citizens. In order to preserve efficient decision-making he suggested that:

> *The voters outside of parliament must respect the division of labour, between themselves and the politicians they elect. They must not withdraw confidence too easily between elections and they must understand that, once they have elected an individual, political action is his business and not theirs. This means that they must refrain from instructing him about what he is to….. All that matters here is that successful democratic practice in great and complicated societies has invariably been hostile to political back-seat driving* (Schumpeter, Capitalism, Socialism and Democracy 1976: 295)

Whether such views are in fact some type of elitist stereotype or do in fact align with the views of many contemporary political 'front seat drivers' is open to question, be they politicians or bureaucrats. On the role of bureaucracy, Weber too shared an elitist perspective on the state and alongside the role of elected elites he also noted the inevitability of bureaucratic expansion leading him to wonder how bureaucratic power might be balanced (Held 1989).

By contrast, advocates of deeper democratic participation consider the more limited, formal, procedural type of democracy described by Schumpeter as being inferior to deeper, more substantive democratic practice in which citizens and their organisations are actively involved in democratic dialogue and decision making. Barber (1984: xi), for example, provides a robust critique of contemporary liberal democracy, claiming that it has "undone democratic institutions" and has made "politics an activity of specialists and experts whose only distinctive qualification, however, turns out to be that they engage in politics". By contrast he argues that "strong democracy is the politics of amateurs where every man is compelled to encounter every other without the intermediary of expertise" (ibid: 152). Participation advocates therefore contend that a healthy democracy requires stronger commitment to deeper, more public and more reasonable democratic debate and dialogue and to the creation of meaningful opportunities for ongoing involvement in decision-making. The papers presented in this volume provide practical analysis, and examples of some efforts to build such deeper democracy.

In practical, policy terms, there are ample sources of apparent support for this more expanded view of public participation. Most notably in Ireland, in 2000 the then government produced a White Paper on Voluntary Activity and the Relationship Between the Community and Voluntary Sector and the State (Government of Ireland 2000) which appeared to lay the basis for a more expanded view of citizen participation. While being careful to preserve the primacy of the elected representative, this policy statement recognised the importance of public participation at a time of rapid social and economic change suggesting that "There is a need to create a more participatory democracy where active citizenship is fostered. In such a society the ability of the Community and Voluntary sector to provide channels for the active involvement and participation of citizens is fundamental". (Government of Ireland 2000: 63). Significantly, not only was there a recognition of the importance of wider participation, there was also an acknowledgement that organised structures within the community and voluntary sector played a key role in channelling such participation. Unfortunately, as has been well documented by Harvey (2004), a subsequent change in ministerial allocations saw the government beat a hasty retreat from the more ambitious and expanded rhetoric of civil society participation towards an apparently more comfortable space of civil society containment.

Some issues about public participation

Clearly, there are a variety of competing perspectives on the merits of public participation, at both a conceptual and a practical level. Realistically, any considerations of the potential for deeper public participation in the formulation and/or implementation of public policy in Ireland need to be conscious of a number of elements.

Re-assessing the role of civil society

Civil society within democratic states is widely accepted as a vital component of a healthy democracy. The Irish Government's own *White Paper on Irish Aid* (Government of Ireland 2006: 41) says quite clearly that an empowered local civil society can, over time, be the most effective driver of political reform and accountability in developing democracies and cites Ireland's own experience as proof that "strong, sustained and equitable economic growth requires a stable and accountable government, substantial sustained investment in education and health, a dynamic and innovative private sector and a strong and vocal civil society". However, an empowered civil society is equally important in so-called developed democracies like Ireland, where there is an acknowledged problem of cynicism towards politics and an increasing distrust of democratic institutions (European Commission 2010a).

When talking about civil society some reminder of what exactly we mean by it is worthwhile. One definition suggests that civil society is:

> *An intermediate realm situated between state and household, populated by organised groups or associations which are separate from the state, enjoy some autonomy in relations with the state and are formed voluntarily by members of society to protect or extend their interests, values or identities (Manor et al. 1999: 201).*

While there are different formulae of words used to describe civil society, this captures its defining features, i.e. that it enjoys both distance and autonomy from the state. Civil society offers an opportunity for citizens to participate in self-organised and largely autonomous associations that engage with the state in a variety of processes ranging from information sharing; devolved service provision or deliberative decision-making. However, the extent and nature of these relationships and the distance between the state and civil society is an area of disagreement, especially where fora of democratic deliberation are largely provided by state institutions and inevitably encourage continued state dominance, such as national social partnership and a variety of local partnership mechanisms.

Others have taken a less enthusiastic view on participation, and do not see engagement with the state as an inevitable function of civil society. Instead, civil society may prioritise changing the terms of political discourse; legitimating different forms of collective action; convening policy oriented fora and generating responses from government as a result of its ability to create political instability (Dryzek 1996: 481). Here, the view is clearly that civil society should be more distinct from the state, thereby ensuring that it flourishes in an oppositional as opposed to a co-operative or co-opting climate, not least if it is to fulfil its potential democratic role.

> *If the impetus for democratisation begins in oppositional civil society rather than in the state - and I would suggest that this has almost always been true historically - then, counter intuitively, a degree of exclusion in the pattern of state interest representation is desirable if civil society and so democracy itself are to flourish (Dryzek 1996: 482).*

The implication here is that civil society should and might well chose to influence policy but that it should do so at a distance from the state, and operate more within 'public spaces' of its own making, such as that created by the *Claiming Our Future* movement. However, in situations where a civil society group chooses to engage, it is argued that "benign inclusion" can only happen when two key conditions are met. Firstly, a group's desired outcomes must be capable of "being assimilated to an established or emerging state imperative" and secondly, "civil society's discursive capacities must not be unduly depleted" (Dryzek 2000: 604). This presents a challenge to organisations seeking to influence public policy in Ireland in a number of ways; how, where it is possible, can the policy priorities of civil society and key state actors be aligned; where alignment is not possible, how can the integrity and capacity of civil society organisations be preserved and not expended on participatory processes that are more cosmetic than real. Thus, in circumstances where inclusion is prescribed or likely to be symbolic at best, it could be argued that civil society led participation should emphasise the creation of autonomous public spaces, away from the state, which may actually contribute more to democratisation. By contrast, pressure for inclusion in public policy processes may well have negative consequences for civil society groups, not least leading to their deradicalisation (Papadopoulos 2003) as a result of being asked to "behave responsibly in governance bodies" (Fung and Wright 2001: 34) but also inducing them to engage in varying degrees of self-censorship.

Power differentials in civil society

Having identified the key defining characteristics of civil society, it is equally important to remind ourselves that this broadly defined concept should not be seen as a homogenous block that operates from shared ideology, analysis or even a shared ideal of the common good. The sphere of civil society clearly includes a whole host of organisations, including community and voluntary sector organisations, trade unions, farming organisations, business alliances, paramilitary groups, religious organisations anti-immigration groups, political parties (in certain circumstances) many of whom may operate from very different and sometimes diametrically opposed ideologies. However, as well as ideological differences a crucial distinction must be drawn on the basis of relative power, control and influence. In particular, the dominant role of the business voice as a component of civil society presents particular problems that potentially impede the realisation of wider citizen participation in policy making and more especially, the ability to address issue of social exclusion. According to Barber (1984: 253-256), there are three particular problems underpinning this concern. Firstly, modern capitalism has generated a "doctrine of economic determinism" which effectively eliminates deliberation on the nature of economic development from the democratic arena. Clearly, social partnership in Ireland operated within a predetermined economic model and in more recent times, the extent of and limits of externally imposed economic policy restrictions is in no doubt. Thus, public policy on a host of issues becomes restricted by ideologically determined economic parameters. On top of this, the "privatistic character of economic individualism" is seen as retarding the potential to identify and deliberate already elusive common or public goods. There is no shortage of commentary on how Ireland's future had been jeopardised by such economic individualism and how public policy outputs facilitated it, while being less open to the types of public goods proposed by community / voluntary sector groups (Connolly 2007). Finally, it is suggested that the very size or "giantism" of the modern multinational corporation itself presents significant challenges to democracy, such that Barber describes the modern corporation as "incompatible with freedom and equality, whether these are construed individually or socially". This radial critique of modern capitalism differs little from that offered by Dahl, a more moderate advocate of pluralist democracy, who went so far as to suggest that the "next great democratic revolution would involve significant restrictions on the freedoms of the market" (Dahl 1989 as cited in Phillips 2004: 69). Clearly, any such prediction is some way off being realised.

Civil society or citizens

Earlier, the links between participation in public policy, active citizenship and the potential role of community and voluntary sector organisations as a channel for communication were noted. However, such linkages cannot be automatically assumed. It is often the case that processes to influence public policy are undertaken through civil society organisations, and do not necessarily involve the direct participation of citizens, or if they do, they do so in a limited way only. The absence of direct involvement thus opens the way to charges that civil society participation is not mandated, is not accountable and ultimately, is not democratically legitimate. In turn, this may lead to efforts by politicians and civil servants to supplement or, perhaps, even replace organisationally oriented participation routes with forms of direct citizen participation, including consultative processes, citizen assemblies, citizen juries and many other that have been developed in recent years (see Smith 2005, for a detailed description of democratic innovations that have emerged in recent years.)

This in turn may lead to the notion of participation by citizens being replaced by an emphasis on participation by 'clients' or 'customers', in keeping with the new public management trend of replicating private sector approaches within the public service.

However, some care does need to be exercised here. Deliberative processes built on individualised participation have only limited capacity to redress power imbalances and may be open to manipulation by a well organised state or other elite interests. In such circumstances, the necessity for stronger collective organisation by citizens is suggested, though the need for stronger mandate and accountability mechanisms cannot be avoided.

State capacity to enable participation

Whatever the mechanisms, there is no doubt that the trend towards participation has placed considerable pressure on state institutions to engage with, and manage, a host of diverse and highly complex relationships. Curiously though, this has resulted in little serious debate on the development of state capacity to support engagement with citizens and/or civil society organisations. So, while the theme of the 2012 annual conference of the American Society for Public Administration is "Redefining Public Service through Civic Engagement", little comparable drive towards enhancing public sector capacity to support deeper civic engagement is visible in Ireland.

It becomes clear that when looking at the capacity needs of any given state, there is a need to talk of a cocktail of capacities, where the development and embedding of economically oriented capacities is matched by the development and embedding of social agenda capacities. Thus, the Irish state has developed considerable capacity to support the transformation of the economy, though the depth of this achievement is less self-evident now than might have been supposed five years ago. However, the state's capacity to address social justice and social policy issues is less obvious, particularly its ability to develop relational and transformative capacities to underpin a more broadly conceived understanding of social justice and democratic participation. This is most acute at the level of the core civil service, which has seen greater reliance on the establishment of specialist agencies (Combat Poverty Agency; the Equality Authority; Family Support Agency etc.) and lesser emphasis on building core competencies in mainstream government departments. At the same time, anecdotal accounts describe how taking on the role of social justice or public participation champion within public sector organisations is not seen as being of any career benefit, thereby curbing enthusiasm for the development of skills in this area. In this regard, it could be argued that bodies such as the IPA and third-level institutions needs to play a stronger role in supporting more rounded public sector capacity building, particularly in deepening knowledge of social justice issues; informing and reshaping individual and institutional dispositions and upgrading the skill sets needed to foster more meaningful participation.

An emerging democratic deficit and prospects for a new outlook

Finally, while the chapters in this book explore some of the ways in which deeper and more sustained public participation might be possible, some caution needs to be noted about threats to both the social justice and civil society infrastructures in Ireland. These arise in the first instance from what appears to be a considered diminution of state commitment to support and engage with civil society organisations that pursue a more overt social justice, advocacy agenda, at both a national and local level. In recent years, some key national organisations have either had their funding substantially reduced or removed entirely. Similarly, at local level programmes such as the Community Development Programme (CDP) have effectively been wound down under the guise of rationalisation and integration with local development structures. In some cases at least, there is no doubt that this has resulted in an abandonment of a prior focus on social inclusion. Compounding this, widespread speculation continues about the potential impact of further integration between local development companies and local government structures. Thus, community based organisations that operated with their own local management structures as part of civil society a relatively short while ago have in most cases disappeared and have been replaced with structures that are increasingly state controlled and/or state located. Where organisations at national and local level continue to receive funding, there is a strong push for them to prioritise service delivery, often at the expense of a policy or democratising role. And while financial pressures are presented as the rationale for these decisions, their democratic impact goes largely unnoticed.

Equally, on the state side specialised social justice agencies, which facilitated civil society, inputs into policy making have also been affected. For example, the Combat Poverty Agency has been 'integrated' into its 'parent' government department, though many of its staff has now been dispersed through other government departments, resulting in significant loss in institutional capacity. There has also been a well-publicised reduction in funding for the Equality Authority its future merger with the Human Rights Commission may potentially result in a loss of capacity and focus.

In the absence of a renewed focus on state capacity one can only suspect that such decisions are likely to lead to a reduction in, rather than a deepening of, public participation in policy making.

CHAPTER 3
A DANCE OF STRANGERS: SOME THOUGHTS ON THE GOVERNMENT - INTEREST GROUP DYNAMIC IN IRISH PUBLIC POLICY FORMULATION

Gary Murphy

Introduction

In early September 2008, the then Minister for Finance, Brian Lenihan TD, in conjunction with his government colleagues decided to bring the 2009 annual budget forward by two months from its traditional December date to one in mid-October. Faced with increasingly grim economic news the budget move was designed to show the Irish people that the government was in control of the fiscal situation and had a plan for dealing with the changed economic realities both in Ireland and across the globe. This decision was to be the prelude to seven months of manic activity where the Government introduced both the normal budget and a supplementary one six months later. An economic plan entitled the *Plan for Economic Renewal* (based on the famous T.K. Whitaker *Economic Development* model of 1958) sank without trace. Government famously guaranteed all the deposits and most crucially, obligations of the privately owned banks in one of the most fateful nights in Irish history.

Government also sundered the social partnership model on which Ireland had run its macro economy since 1987. That final decision, taken in February 2009, was crucial in bringing to an end a period of formal interest group involvement in the public policy formulation of decision making in the Irish state which had dated back to early 1960s. The aim of this chapter is to assess the relationship between governments and interest groups as the state directed economic policy with increased input from such sectional interests over a half century from the late 1950s to the end of the first decade of the twenty first century. It argues that while these actors (farmers, trade unions and business associations) were co-opted by the state to be partners in a type of managed economic democracy, governments have not hesitated to side-line them when they perceived that the views of certain interests impeded what government took to be national economic priorities.

The Proto Corporate State

Involving the main interest groups in the policy process had been a central element of Irish economic policy making from the time Seán Lemass became Taoiseach in 1959. It was during this era that the economic interests were invited to participate in the work of a number of national bodies that were concerned with formulating a new approach to economic management (Horgan 1997: 228–49; Murphy 2003: 105–18). This approach co-ordinated by Lemass had as its ultimate aim entry to the European Economic Community. It was with this goal in mind and the perceived need to show a united front to western Europe, at a time when Ireland was only just coming out of a deep recession and was viewed internationally as a small agricultural economy on the European periphery, that the economic interest groups were co-opted into this tripartite arrangement towards economic management (Murphy 2009a). The Lemass governments of the early 1960s had actively sought the input of unions, employers and farmers organisations, in what was effectively a realignment of government economic policy which placed agricultural and industrial policy on an equal footing for the first time in the history of the state. The Employer-Labour (ELC) conference came into existence in 1962 and the National Industrial and Economic Council was established a year later. These new agencies paralleled the state's commitment to economic planning and in 1964 the National Farmers' Association received formal government recognition in connection with the formulation of state agricultural policy. In essence this meant that the Government would not devise any new agricultural policies or initiatives without first interacting with the representatives of organised farming.

By 1970, however, with Fianna Fáil having twice failed to take Ireland into the EEC in 1963 and again in 1967, under the objections, principally to the British application, of Charles de Gaulle and with the various political parties, the trade union movement and the employers' organisations frustrated by the very fractious nature of industrial relations, there was uncertainty as to the political implications of the breakdown of Lemass's proto corporate state. For breakdown, it most certainly had. The Lemassian structure where all sides sat together inside the charmed circle of power and attempted to thrash out some sort of macroeconomic agreement had not brought peace and stability to the economic situation as envisaged by Lemass when he set about to bring the economic interest groups into the tent of national policy making. Instead it brought industrial relations gridlock.

Such gridlock had a significant economic impact. By 1970 the rate of inflation was running at about 8.5 per cent. The *Irish Times* pointed out that the improvements in living standards that had been earned in the 1960s, the principal reason for Lemass's initiatives, were in danger of being lost due to such inflation.[1] At a national level the Economic and Social Research Institute noted that the statistics for industrial output, employment, volume of imports, and retail sales all indicated economic stagnation, while internationally the Organisation for European Cooperation and Development argued that "this was partly due to the direct and indirect effects of labour disputes" (Murphy and Hogan 2008: 580). In such a context economic crisis resulting from a rising level of industrial conflict and forceful trade union wage pressure ultimately forced the government to adopt a more interventionist approach.

The consequence of the free for all pay round system of the 1960s was to imperil attempts to control and centralise collective bargaining. Industrial relations deteriorated in the late 1960s and the daily news was dominated by major industrial confrontations. The high level of industrial conflict in 1969 and 1970 was widely regarded as representing a crisis in collective bargaining as the unions and employers had failed to reach agreement on incomes policy. With stagnating production appearing alongside a price and wage explosion, economic conditions deteriorated during the course of 1970. The combination of relatively slow growth, strong inflation and a large current external deficit presented a dilemma for economic policy makers (Murphy and Hogan 2008: 581). A large balance of payments deficit imposed significant constraints on the degree of expansion that could be permitted. As prices became the primary concern of the Government, the budgetary strategy was aimed at moderating the rise in government spending so as not to contribute to inflation. Another lesson from the 1960s was the need for a joint body to administer the national pay agreements. It was against this background of industrial strife and economic difficulties that the National Industrial and Economic Council prepared its *Report on Incomes and Prices Policy* which

---

[1] *The Irish Times*, 12th October, 1970.

regarded economic expansion and decentralised collective bargaining as incompatible. A consequence of this was the reconstitution of the ELC in May 1970. This was significant in the long-term restructuring of the adversarial conduct of industrial relations as the government became a participant in the ELC due to the increasing standoff between unions and employers in terms of the rates of pay increases for employees in both the public and private sector.

For its part, the Fianna Fáil government of Jack Lynch was becoming increasingly worried by the ongoing situation. In such a context the failure of the ELC to produce any agreement to moderate pay resulted in the government's decision to take action by introducing statutory controls on wages and salaries on a prices and incomes bill, as otherwise a vacuum would be created into which the unions would most likely come with increasingly exorbitant pay claims (Murphy and Hogan, 2008: 582). The bill was justified by Fianna Fáil on the grounds of the grossly accelerated rate of price increases, with the Minister for Finance, George Colley, arguing that it was being introduced with "the purpose of safeguarding the economy, in the national interest, from the present serious dangers threatening it".[2] He pointed out that the government would have much preferred a programme of voluntary restraint on incomes when it was so obviously vital to the national wellbeing, but it was clear that Lemass's proto corporate state had not persuaded the employers' groups and the trade unions to come together in a harmonious approach to macroeconomic policy making. If anything, being inside the policy making tent had made it easier for both groups to adopt a more intransigent strategy on the grounds that they were indispensable to the State by dint of their place at the policy making table.

Ultimately, the threat of this legislation resulted in the first national agreement for six years in December 1970, notwithstanding the Irish Congress of Trade Unions' (ICTU) opposition to being coerced into a deal and its advocacy of free collective bargaining (Weinz 1986: 98). ICTU felt, however, that it had little choice but to sign up to what it saw as the Government's dictat; the alternative was to be left out in the cold. This proved a watershed of sorts in that it precipitated the dismantling of the boundary separating politics and industrial relations (Roche, 1989). With active state involvement in industrial relations came direct

---

[2] Dáil Debates, Vol. 249, col. 54, 28th October 1970.

trade union involvement in public policy making. By the mid 1970s, the new collective bargaining approach was to be marked by quid pro quo arrangements on taxation issues between unions and the state.

Yet in the 1970s, the focus of state policy shifted; corporatist policies in the economic sphere were dropped and the process was no longer directly aided by governmental financial support (Hardiman 1988). Notwithstanding this, the continuing high level of state intervention in the economy ensured an ongoing and important role for the Confederation of Irish Industry (McCann 1993: 51). To a lesser degree, this was also the case with the trade unions and the farmers' organisations. While the sectional groups were not central to economic decision making, they were far from isolated voices in the wilderness. The trade union movement in particular in this period was seen by all governments as a type of expedient friend who could be brought into the charmed circle of power and then brusquely dismissed when circumstances changed (Murphy and Hogan 2008: 596). During the 1970s, governments tended to oscillate between supporting negotiations with the trade unions and sustaining voluntary employer-labour agreements on the one hand and threatening statutory controls on the other. The threat to legislate on a statutory pay norm was sometimes used to hasten a 'voluntary agreement' – this deriving mostly out of economic necessity.

1987: A New Dynamic

The centrality of the role of the social partners in economic policy making has differed over time. The process of social partnership put in place by the Fianna Fáil minority government in 1987 for instance was notably different from the pay agreements of the 1970s. When Fianna Fáil returned to office in 1987 it decided that the route back to prosperity would be through a new type of agreement between government and the social partners. During the 1987 election campaign, following five years of economic hardship under a Fine Gael - Labour government, Fianna Fáil had stressed its traditional commitment to economic growth via social partnership. Facing a grave fiscal crisis, the new minority Fianna Fáil government, acting in conjunction with the social partners, agreed a strategy to overcome Ireland's economic difficulties based on the premise of partnership whereby the sectional interests would negotiate with the Government in a process of economic governance.

This approach ultimately evolved into a system that aimed to keep all the major interests reasonably happy by giving them a role within the broad economic approach of the State, which in turn was to perpetuate a type of national economic and social coalition. This consensual approach mirrored that of northern European social democracies such as Sweden, Norway and Denmark, all of whom of course were economic success stories that the new Fianna Fáil government looked to as models of economic governance. While a new relationship developed between the social partners in both the early and late 1970s, this was largely based on terms established by the Government and then brusquely terminated when it suited the new economic strategy of fiscal restraint in the early 1980s.

The social partnership process put in place in 1987 was also flexible and adjustable but in a significantly different manner from earlier agreements in that Fianna Fáil genuinely looked upon the sectional groups as full social partners whose participation was vital to securing the long term future and viability of the Irish state. This is no exaggeration. Ireland in 1987 was a state in depression with huge unemployment, massive emigration and a people with little hope. Acting in the tripartite National Economic and Social Council (NESC), the social partners agreed a strategy to overcome Ireland's economic difficulties. The NESC's *Strategy For Development* (1986) formed the basis upon which, in 1987, the new Fianna Fáil government and the social partners negotiated the social partnership programme known as the *Programme for National Recovery*. This would be followed by six other agreements. What made these agreements different from those of the 1960s and 1970s was that they were not simply centralised wage mechanisms but agreements on a wide range of economic and social policies such as tax reform and the evolution of welfare payments (O'Donnell and Thomas 1998: 118).

With the development of the *Partnership 2000* agreement in 1996, a watershed was reached as for the first time agencies from the voluntary sector - including charities and self-help groups - were included in consultation and ultimately negotiations. This agreement was negotiated by a Fine Gael – Labour government as distinct from a Fianna Fáil government, which is interesting in itself in that Fine Gael in particular were critical of social partnership agreements while in opposition on the grounds that they removed democratically elected politicians (i.e. the opposition) from engaging in the macroeconomic management of the state which they said was managed by the government in an unholy alliance with unelected interest groups. However, on returning to power in 1994, after the collapse of the Fianna Fáil – Labour government, Fine Gael were persuaded by Labour that social partnership was essential to the macroeconomic management of the State and they quickly set about negotiating what would become Partnership 2000.

This new initiative resulted from complaints that the Government and the economic partners were missing an opportunity to tackle social exclusion in an integrated fashion by ignoring the voices of other interest groups. The most graphic illustration of this widening of the social partnership parameters was the inclusion of the Irish National Organisation of the Unemployed in the negotiations – the first time that the unemployed had been seen by the Government as an actor with something to offer to social partnership negotiation.[3] In that context, what Partnership 2000 looked forward to was nothing less than the enactment of a new social contract. Yet the voluntary organisations found themselves lower down in the hierarchy of interests and were clearly ranked below business and labour showing very clearly that in social partnership it was the employers and the unions who remained the pivotal actors. The voluntary actors found themselves marginalised and sidelined but took the view, for the most part, that it was better to be inside the partnership tent where they could at least attempt to influence policy as distinct from being outside shouting in.

June 2006 saw the publication of the seventh social partnership agreement, *Towards 2016*, which, according to the government, developed a new framework to address key social challenges which focused on the needs of children, young adults, people of working age, older people and people with disabilities. To this end the agreement explicitly placed issues such as diversity, immigration and the repositioning of Ireland's social policies at its core.[4]

---

[3] http://www.taoiseach.gov.ie/eng/Publications/Publications_Archive/Publications_2006/Publications_for_1998/Partnership_2000.html
[4] See Towards 2016: Ten year framework social partnership agreement 2006-2015 online at http://www.taoiseach.gov.ie/attached_files/Pdf%20files/Towards2016PartnershipAgreement.pdf

The most significant aspect of the social partnership agreements was that they gave both the Government and the social partners a remarkable twenty years of continuity in economic macro-management and certainly helped in abating the dire economic crisis of the mid 1980s. Nevertheless, it is important to note that these types of partnership agreements had the tendency to be only as good as their last deal. In that context it is significant to note that each successive agreement had become increasingly more difficult to negotiate. For instance, the linked pay deal agreed in September 2008 was only reached after mammoth negotiations which were described as the toughest in the twenty years of pay talks since social partnership began. Then came the momentous decision to guarantee the banks in the early hours of 30 September 2008. By the time the Government issued its *Plan for Economic Renewal* in December 2008 the voices seeking a reworking of the partnership deal had reached heights unheard of since the first agreement in 1987.

The End of Partnership

In December 2008, the Fianna Fáil, Green, Progressive Democrat coalition government presented to the public their plan to deal with the increasingly grim economic crisis of 2008. Informally titled the *Plan for Economic Renewal* it was the Government's response to six months of catastrophic economic news after over a decade of boom of which the twin processes of social partnership and EU membership were seen as pillars of the country's economic success. Amongst a number of initiatives, the plan called for heavy investment in research and development which would incentivise multinational companies to locate more such capacity in Ireland, ensuring the commercialisation and retention of ideas that flowed from that investment. Two months earlier, Minister for Finance, Brian Lenihan, had issued the 2009 budget which he described as nothing less than a call to patriotic action to face the deterioration in the Government's fiscal position. The 2009 budget was introduced in, as Lenihan put it, one of the most "difficult and uncertain times in living memory" where the global credit crunch had created turmoil in the world's financial markets and steep increases in commodity prices placed enormous pressures on economies across the globe, including Ireland.[5] The financial position in 2009 was completely

---

[5] http://www.budget.gov.ie/2009/financialstatement.html

different to what any Irish government had faced in a generation. The dark days of the 1980s had been replaced by a period of economic boom which had pretty much lasted through the two terms of the Fianna Fáil – Progressive Democrats government from 1997 to 2007. Bertie Ahern, who had led Fianna Fáil to election triumphs in 1997, 2002 and 2007, had no doubt that social partnership was instrumental not only to Fianna Fáil's success, and he was the principal political architect of the process, but also to the success of the country. As he wrote in June 2006 in his introduction to the *Towards 2016* social partnership agreement:

> *Social Partnership has helped to maintain a strategic focus on key national priorities, and has created and sustained the conditions for remarkable employment growth, fiscal stability, restructuring of the economy to respond to new challenges and opportunities, a dramatic improvement in living standards, through both lower taxation and lower inflation, and a culture of dialogue, which has served the social partners, but more importantly, the people of this country, very well.*

The very semblance of a threat from any of the social partners to withdraw from one of the agreements usually precipitated intense discussions to ensure that the demands of the sector were met without jeopardising the remit of the agreements as a whole. But social partnership for all its success was showing significant signs of wear and tear as the economy went into its downward spiral in late 2008. Nevertheless, in the *Plan for Economic Renewal* the Taoiseach Brian Cowen renewed his government's commitment to social partnership noting that it was the Government's intention to work with the social partners on the development and implementation of the plan, which was consistent with the principles and vision underpinning *Towards 2016*, using the well-established mechanisms of the social partnership process.

Social Partnership was the structure by which the Irish State governed itself from 1987 to just after the economic tsunami hit Ireland in the second half of 2008 when the financial crisis saw the Irish banks literally become insolvent. As Peter Stafford points out, the truth was that the real work was done by a small set of people, while many of the members of both unions and employers remained sidelined on the fringes of power (Stafford 2011: 78). Over twenty years of social partnership led, however, to a corrosion of intellectual thinking in Irish policy making whereby no-one in power seemed to have even the slightest idea of what to do once the economy started to go into freefall after the boom years of the Celtic Tiger ended (Murphy and McGrath 2011: 71). Once the depth and gravity of the economic crisis became ever more clear the social partners, particularly the trade unions and employers, retreated into a behavioural pattern that was akin to that of the 1960s by lobbying for resources rather than acting as partners in a search for a way out of the economic morass that the country found itself in. The social partnership process was unable to react to the crisis except through a return to a simple, but woefully outdated, wage bargaining process (Stafford 2011: 78).

This retreat, however, had a significant political impact as it exposed a major breach in Fianna Fáil between the Taoiseach, Brian Cowen, and his Minister for Finance, Brian Lenihan. In February 2009, just two months after the *Plan for Economic Renewal*, Cowen announced yet another plan; this time titled a *Framework for Stabilisation, Social Solidarity, and Economic Renewal*. Cowen desperately wanted the trade unions to sign up to this framework, but ICTU decided that they could not support it. The Government, particularly on the urgings of Lenihan, who had long since come to the conclusion that social partnership as a mechanism could not deal with the gravity of the economic crisis, decided to push ahead without the unions and so ended the two and a half decade long experiment of social partnership. One commentator has argued that the government took a political risk by taking what were basically macroeconomic management decisions without backing from one of the main social partners (Masters 2009: 142). And while there is certainly some truth in this it is probably as accurate to say that the risk was pretty negligible due to the fact that the trade union movement had very little public support for its wage bargaining position. Most public opinion viewed the trade union movement as being in existence to principally protect cosseted public service workers in what was mainly a private sector economic recession. And while there can be no doubt that the public service was deeply affected through pay cuts and income levies, the trade union movement was unable to respond within a social partnership forum beyond lobbying for more resources in what was a shrinking market. In any event, once the Government had to access the EU/ECB/IMF bailout in November 2010 to fund the country, social partnership had proved to be very much a straw man in the Irish context as the Fianna Fáil – Green Party's unwelcome dance partners became the Troika who provided the bailout facility to keep the Irish economy afloat.

Social partnership began and ended in two separate and equally grim economic recessions in 1987 and 2008. As a prototype of how to manage an economy it dated back to the ending of another recession at the close of the 1950s. The sectional interest groups have long enjoyed close and even privileged access to the charmed circles of power of Leinster House. However, what the lesson of this latest grim crisis tells us is that if these interest groups cannot proffer proactive solutions beyond their own narrow sectional base then governments will move forward without them and will change dance partners in attempts to find solutions to economic collapse.

CHAPTER 4
EMBEDDING COMMUNITY PARTICIPATION IN LOCAL PUBLIC POLICY MAKING: REVIEWING THE IRISH EXPERIENCE 1991-2012

Deiric Ó Broin

Introduction

There is a well-established literature on the case for community participation in public policy making but very little discussion of community involvement in Irish public policy making processes, particularly at local level. The experience of local communities engaged in dialogue with state-directed local development agencies provides a useful case study. This article will examine how the Irish state has attempted to structure community involvement in public policy making and to assess the state's efforts to embed local development actions within communities.

This chapter has six distinct components. Section 1 outlines the article's primary research objectives[6] while Section 2 discusses how the relationship between democratic theory and public policy in the area of local development is rather diffuse and the implications for public policy of developing policy initiatives based on vague and poorly constructed premises. Section 3 outlines findings as they relate to national public policy and Section 4 examines how it relates to public policy formation at local level. Section 5 presents the main findings of the research and Section 6 presents recommendations.

Research objectives

There remain significant gaps in our understanding of the relationship between democratic theory, public policy formulation and institutional design, particularly at local level. These gaps provide the parameters for the following research question: Has the state actively facilitated community involvement in public policy decision-making as it relates to the actions of local development agencies? In particular, what can be learned from the experience of community involvement with local

---

[6] The article is based on a research project carried out in the Centre for Co-operative Studies in UCC and the findings have been updated to include changes in policy as of July 2012.

development agencies and the impact of state actions on this experience? These overall aims lead to a number of more specific objectives for this chapter, namely to examine the relevant democratic theory literature; the Irish public policy framework for community involvement; the role of relevant Departmental guidelines and directives on community involvement in local development agencies; possible reforms to strengthen the existing mechanisms community involvement.

Democratic theory and local development public policy

An examination of how public participation is addressed in political theory, while limited, raises a number of issues pertinent to public policy formulation:

- Citizens and communities participate in public policy processes for a variety of reasons;
- If the state wants its invitation for participation to be accepted and embedded in community based processes then the state's rationale for those invitations must be cogent and coherent;
- As Fung and Wright argue, the current institutional architecture of liberal democratic states is ineffective in accomplishing the central ideas of democratic politics, i.e. facilitating active political involvement by citizens, forging political consensus through dialogue, devising and implementing public policies that embed a productive economy and healthy society (2003: 3).

The Irish state will have to re-examine, in a coherent manner, how it structures its relationship with local communities.

National public policy and community involvement

A number of significant obstacles exist to embedding local development actions within communities, in particular through developing appropriate community participation mechanisms. These include the apparent conflict between state actions and rhetoric, power struggles between the local state and central state, public representatives and communities, and within communities. In addition the discourse in this area is often incoherent. A meaningful debate addressing the relationship between citizens, communities and the state, while central to clarifying what is meant by community participation and the various beliefs and premises that underpin this participation, is largely absent in the Irish setting.

The Green Paper on Local Government Reform (Government of Ireland 2008) contains a chapter entitled "Participative Democracy and Local Government". This contains a variety of proposals to facilitate community participation, including "petition rights, participatory budgeting, town meetings and plebiscites" (2008: 79). Two significant problems arise from the analysis contained within the report. First, while it largely follows the perspective of the Report of the Taskforce on Active Citizenship (2007) and discusses the impact of civic republicanism on its deliberations, the report remains silent on the developmental versus protective debate. This is a major omission as it is possible to be a civic republican and believe in participation in order to protect my rights because I don't trust the institutions of the state not to try and dominate me or usurp my rights (Cicero [51BC] 2009 and Pettit 1999), and equally possible to be a civic republican who believes that participation will make me a better citizen (Sandel 1996). If the state can't cogently articulate why its citizens should participate, what hope is there that the mechanisms it develops to operationalise this participation will be effective?

A second problem with the Green Paper (2008) and the Taskforce Report (2007) is the continuation of similar language and recommendations in the Green Paper (1997) and White Paper (2000) on supporting voluntary activity, the Reports of the Taskforce on the Integration of Local Development and Local Government Systems (1998-2001) and the even older Better Local Government Report (1996). Similar language was evident at the launch of the Poverty III Programme (1987) or the Community Development Programme (1990). Clearly there is a state rhetoric available to be rolled out when necessary however the ability and willingness of agencies of the state to operationalise this rhetoric tends to be absent.

Local public policy and community involvement

The first finding in the local sphere relates to a lack of coherence in policy formulation and implementation. In the early stages of the local development agencies' programme, 1991-1993, the approach adopted to facilitate community participation was top-down. It paid little attention to local sensitivities. This was followed by what might be called a period of 'benign neglect' as local development agencies were allowed to develop the mechanisms that they saw fit, 1994-1999. From approximately 2000 there appears to have been a change in perspective and the introduction of target group representatives was now perceived to be of key importance. It is understood that this has its roots in what Pestoff refers to as 'participationalism' (2009: 203), i.e. citizens should "engage personally in shaping the welfare services they demand". However as Murray and Rogers point out this approach has had a number of negative consequences (2009: 129).

The expansion of the areas in which local development companies operate in the 2007-2009 period meant that the mechanisms championed by Pobal in the 2000-2006 period now had to be revisited. The new extended areas, however, by the nature of their socio-economic composition often lacked groups targeted for representation. This in turn led to the adoption by many local development agencies of the community forum model. In addition to the lack of a coherent policy on community participation, there were distinct changes to the composition of the boards of local development agencies in 2009, and changes in models of community participation supported by Pobal. The experience of many local development agencies is that the state has consistently underestimated the support necessary to involve communities in any meaningful manner: In the words of one research interviewee:

> ... Volunteers' expenses are eligible for development boards to pay and that removes some barriers such as childcare restrictions or travel costs.... there are issues with participation that makes involvement in the decision-making process challenging for community members. There is a huge reliance upon technology in order to participate in decision making, access to e-mail in order to keep up to date is essential and many people don't have this knowledge or resources to access e-mail regularly. So many funding streams are complicated and time intensive and if involved in the process, an expectation of a knowledge of "expert language" is assumed during discussions in order to facilitate saving time but new members are restricted from participating due to a lack of knowledge....Community members are not always fully aware of what they are signing up for due to a lack of clear role descriptions around their involvement....there are difficulties with the representative feeding the information back to the community adequately as it is very time consuming process to do so.

Furthermore, the research has identified the apparent lack of consultation between the Department of Community, Rural and

Gaeltacht Affairs (DCRAGA), Pobal and the local development agencies as a major problem. For example, in April 2007 DCRAGA insisted that it would reserve the right to appoint the Chairpersons of the various boards, despite the fact that each of the local development companies already had sitting chairpersons. Furthermore the right to appoint the independent chairpersons had been a prerogative of the boards since 1991. DCRAGA reversed its decision in October 2007. In addition DCRAGA unilaterally decided to reduce the size of the social partner component of the boards from 6-8 to 2 representatives. This was done without consultation with the social partners. Neither ICTU nor IBEC were contacted by DCRAGA prior to the decision. The decision was reversed in October 2007. An analysis of the various memoranda and discussion between DCRAGA and the integrated local development companies' representatives shows the initial lack of concern at the local development company's views about these changes. It was only when the legal and political ramifications of a number of these were outlined that DCRAGA reversed its decisions.

From the outset the state's efforts to involve local communities in its' local development programmes has been beset with problems. Ireland had and retains a culture and mindset of public service centralisation. As one research participant observed "It is not used to consulting'. Furthermore its policy design process has not addressed a number of key questions, e.g. why do citizens participate? Why should they participate and how should the state facilitate participation? By choosing not to address these issues, policies have been devised and mechanisms implemented that are, in reality, designed to fail. They could not become embedded in the social relations of local communities because they took no account of the social relations of local communities. What limited successes that have been achieved have been based on effectively sidestepping departmental requirements.

Key findings

The key findings are presented using the following framework; democratic theory and public policy; public policy at national level; public policy at local level.

The relationship between abstract democratic theory and public policy may, at first sight, appear tenuous however the clarity and coherence inherent in democratic theory constitutes useful perspectives from which to examine public policy formulation. The case of community/citizen participation policy in Ireland is particularly interesting. This article contends that there is a lack of clarity underpinning Irish public policy in this area, for example, the lack of examination of fundamental questions such as why citizens or communities should participate, why they actually participate, and why the state asks them to participate. Despite a review of modern literature in this area, e.g. Taskforce on Active Citizenship, the analysis avoids addressing these, and related, questions.

With regard to public policy at national level, two key findings emerge. Despite the presence of a number of common themes running through the last decade and a half there remains a lack of clarity as to why citizens and communities are expected to participate. Despite a significant number of policy documents being drafted and published, it is very difficult to identify concrete and coherent actions the state has undertaken to make manifest its stated commitment to citizen/community participation, or to develop new "avenues of participation and communication between local authorities and the communities they represent" that "could allow citizens to exercise a greater degree of control over local services and facilities" (Government of Ireland 2008: 80).

In terms of public policy at local level there is a lack of consultation between the Department of Community, Rural and Gaeltacht Affairs (DCRAGA), Pobal and the local development agencies.

The second finding in the area relates to the lack of consideration given to the implications of expanding the local development companies' areas of operation and the communities they would now be working with. In addition to the lack of foresight in this matter it was found that DCRAGA did not engage in any meaningful consultation exercise with the local development companies or their representatives. Despite this lack of consultation and the problems and delays that arose from this during the implementation of these new mechanisms, the relevant Minister castigated the integrated local development companies for delays in electing community directors (MacConnell 2008b, 2008c and 2008d).

Recommendations for public policy

Recommendations can best be categorised in two areas, (a) a national or inter-departmental sphere, and (b) a DCRAGA/Pobal/integrated local development company sphere. With regard to the former a number of fundamental issues need to be addressed. These include mapping out previous state commitments to facilitating community participation and reviewing how these have been implemented or if not implemented the various obstacles identified to their implementation. Once this exercise is completed it is recommended that the state should examine how it can oversee the implementation of current initiatives, e.g. those contained in the Green Paper on Local Government Reform *Stronger Local Democracy – Options for Change* (2008), in the context of its previous failures. These will be a major exercise as it will involve a substantial element of inter-departmental co-operation.

With regard to the DCRAGA/Pobal/integrated local development company sphere, the analysis of documentation and interview data portrays an image of a very dysfunctional area of public policy formulation. The appropriate relationships between DCRAGA, Pobal and the local development agencies require more clarity.

In addition, the amalgamation of the LEADER Companies and the Area and Community Partnerships has given rise to an interesting anomaly. In terms of LEADER funding the integrated local development company deals directly with the Department of Agriculture, Food and Fisheries and, indirectly, the EU, but the funding provided under the new Local and Community Development Programme (LDCP) involves dealing with Pobal, as the funding intermediary, and DCRAGA as the parent department dealing with such issues as governance. When one includes funding from the Health Service Executive, FÁS, Rural Social Scheme, Whole Time Job Initiative, County/City Enterprise Boards and private funding from organisations like Atlantic Philanthropies, reporting relationships can become complex very quickly. As a result integrated local development companies have to deal with a variety of funding agencies in a variety of ways and this complexity tends to be disregarded by DCRAGA (Ó Broin 2009).

Finally the resources required to facilitate community participation from marginalised communities and non-marginalised communities are often underestimated (Ó Broin 2009; Murray and Rogers 2009: 127). In addition when cutbacks are advertised the first budget that tends to be cut is that allocated to community capacity building. Again it is recommended that, despite the current financial situation, the relationships between DCRAGA, Pobal and the integrated local development companies need to be placed on a coherent and sustainable footing. It is not conducive to effective planning and service delivery if the level of autonomy granted to integrated local development companies, all of which are legally independent, is subject to official whim.

One of the most interesting aspects of this research is the relative paucity of existing material in the area of the relationship between elected public representatives, in particular city/county/town councillors and the locally elected directors of integrated local development companies. The author is aware that among the boards of directors of the Dublin integrated local development companies in the late-1990s this was an issue, primarily because the local councillors were prevented from sitting on boards of local development agencies. This situation changed in 1999 and since then each local development company has had councillors on its board. There are obvious issues of contestation and conflict between two classes of elected representative, e.g. legitimacy and representativeness. Since January 2009 this has become even more interesting as locally elected directors are currently on the boards of local development agencies that operate on a countywide basis. As a result elected directors can now have countywide representative duties. The authors are not aware of any research in this area at this time.

The relationship between integrated local development companies and the state is problematic, in particular between Pobal and the Department of Community, Rural and Gaeltacht Affairs (DCRAGA). Are the integrated local development companies agents of the state or independent limited liability companies contracted to deliver certain services? The *Guidelines* issued by DCRAGA in April and October 2007 raise a significant number of questions about the power of the relevant minister to influence the decisions of locally-constituted and legally independent boards. This area is, to the researcher's knowledge, largely unexplored.

Conclusion

In summary the area of public policy as it relates to community participation in local development actions is still evolving. At the time of writing significant changes to the Irish local development sector are proposed. It is unclear what implications arise for the sector, unlike many of our EU counterparts Ireland has yet to develop robust and coherent models of community participation (Ó Broin and Waters 2007: 32-34). In addition to the absence of such mechanisms attempts by integrated local development companies have been *ad-hoc*. A key aspect of this relates to the lack of coherent national policy in this area. Despite approximately 20 years of policy documents and the local development agencies being in existence since 1991 the implementation of policy has been weak. This largely relates to a seeming unwillingness on the part of the state to implement appropriate mechanisms. Despite the success of some integrated local development companies and their efforts to establish models of good practice, changing departmental guidelines have meant that these successes rarely become embedded. As a result the state's efforts to embed community participation in local development actions has not been a success and is unlikely to be until the state can devise, implement and maintain a coherent policy initiative in this area.

CHAPTER 5
A CASE OF CONCEPT STRETCHING?
AN ANALYSIS OF THE INTRODUCTION OF ASSET-BASED COMMUNITY DEVELOPMENT (ABCD) IN DUBLIN CITY

Matthias Borscheid

Introduction

In 2008, Dublin City Council (DCC), piloted a new neighbourhood development model centred on Asset-Based Community Development (ABCD). ABCD is rooted in the assumption of 'potentiality' which assumes that people, based on their capacity to identify and mobilise local social capital and resources, will act upon issues that they care about and thereby ameliorate levels of disadvantage and achieve betterment of quality of life for people in the community (McKnight 1996). This article reviews a case study of DCC's *2008-12 Community and Neighbourhood Development Strategy* (Strategy) and an ABCD pilot which took place in Dublin City Council (DCC) over the period 2008-2012. The article first introduces ABCD and then reviews the chronological journey of ABCD in DCC, from its first ideational conception to its practical application in DCC's community and neighbourhood development strategy in Dublin. The analysis points to tensions. On the one hand, some might interpret ABCD as a neighbourhood revitalisation model designed to assist the local authority in achieving its own governance objectives. On the other hand, it might be seen as an enabling instrument fostering the empowerment of communities and a genuine attempt to allow for the genuine development of a new, citizen-led model of community participation in decision-making. The article concludes an adjusted ABCD could possibly make a positive contribution.

What is ABCD?

Supporters of ABCD consider mobilisation of local assets by communities the key ingredient for addressing manifestations of poverty in areas affected by socio-economic disadvantage and political marginalisation. Assets here are understood as social capital and individual skills; organised interest groups/associations; institutions and agencies; physical assets such as building, funding and property; and connections and networks that facilitate exchange between people (Kretzmann and McKnight 1993). ABCD is critical of local development models that depend on statutory resource-provision and/or rely on the delivery of community-based services via the institutionalised state-funded local/community development sector. It is argued that these create a dependency of local people on external supports and services whereby they "become consumers of services, with no incentives to become producers" (Kretzmann and McKnight 1993: 2). The managing director of Nurture Development Limited (hereafter NDL), a private company that has been actively involved in the development of the Strategy in Dublin and that promotes ABCD in Ireland and internationally (Nurture Development Website[7]), argues an implicit ABCD approach dominated the Irish Community and Voluntary (C+V) landscape until it was replaced in the 1960s by an increasingly state-funded professionalised sector that prioritised a needs-oriented approach.

Potentiality

ABCD has to be understood in the context of tensions between redistributive and market-driven policies which intensified throughout the 1990s neoliberal era of restructuring the social and economic policies of the state. The shift towards privatisation of state assets, contractual outsourcing of state services and the partial withdrawal from, and privatisation of, welfare provision and social security was accompanied by two trends: firstly, an individualisation of responsibility for failure and success (Harvey 2005); secondly, a redefinition of social transfers and public expenditures as investments that need to yield maximum returns, enhance economic participation and contribute to increasing economic competitiveness. Policies and programmes promoting wealth redistribution and welfare have been traded off against those supporting workfare, economic potency and competitiveness of places. This means an increasing focus on cities as engines of national growth (McGuirk 2003; Scott 2006) and emphasis on endogenous, place-specific, assets and a flexible, multi-level governance to manage emerging social, economic and policy interests *at various spatial scales* (Amin and Thrift 1995; Healey 2006). Scott and

---

[7] Accessed on January 30th 2012 at http://www.nurturedevelopment.ie/

Storper (2003: 586) highlight "that regional economic development involves a mixture of exogenous constraints, the re-organization and *build-up of local asset systems*, and political mobilization focused on institutions, socialization and social capital" (emphasis added).

The focus on *potentiality* is a useful framework for the analysis of the introduction of ABCD in Dublin as it influences the ideological orientation of contemporary urban regeneration policies and city governance (MacLaran and Williams 2003; Peck 2007). *Potentiality* refers to the latent capacity of people and places to stimulate and progress developments leading to positive changes locally that, in turn, can sustainably influence structural forces that have been adversely impacting on an area. Local development approaches that follow the core principles of ABCD can be considered an opportunity that acknowledges the scope for local bottom-up initiatives based on participatory democracy and genuine involvement of citizens in being part of developing places and shaping policies – *irrespective of socio-political or economic disparities*. Figure 1 illustrates three possible scenarios or implementation modes for ABCD (Modes 1-3).

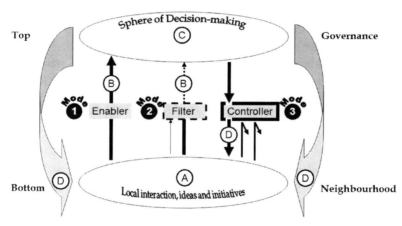

The diagram shows the 3 Modes of the ABCD model in dealing with communities:

(1) Enabler (Emancipatory)
(2) Filter (Inverse-care Law)
(3) Controller (Manipulative)

The diagram above illustrates that there is a dynamic process of interaction at play between the Governance Structure (at the top) and the locale (at the bottom).
(A) Mobilising local people, ideas or assets
(B) Bottom-up transfer and penetration of (some) ideas into the Sphere of Decision-making
(C) Decision-making processes
(D) Top-down actions and their impact on the local area

If ABCD follows the *inverse care law (Mode 2)* or is deployed as an *instrument of managerial control (Mode 3)*, then little influence can be exerted from the bottom up.

Figure 1: Operational Modes of ABCD[8]

Promoters of ABCD argue it is a policy framework that allows both rich *and* poor places to release their development *potential*. This requires ABCD to be implemented in a spirit of creativity and potentiality and with a fluid, flexible and responsive approach that takes emerging local ideas seriously and works as a capacity-building tool enabling local people in communities to explore the potential of their neighbourhood and support the development of ideas (Mode 1) It is acknowledged the approach could also fall victim to an *inverse-care law* (Pringle 1999) where support is directed to the most competitive places that have the potential to become winners and yield the best possible return for money and support invested (Mode 2). This is not necessarily a bad approach *per se* - especially when public resources for local development are limited; though areas that already have higher levels of social capital and economic resources are more likely to mobilise assets, engage with decision-makers and exert influence that areas that are less resourceful. Another potential faultline is the deployment of ABCD as an instrument to *exert managerial control* over places and direct investments into a pre-defined pattern that is considered desirable by political sponsors or initiators of the approach (Mode 3). The case study tests which of these three scenarios might apply.

How it arrived: Navigating toward ABCD

The case study of ABCD in DCC takes place in a specific Irish context. Contemporary neoliberal policies pursue the development of economic opportunities based on the concept of potentiality of places. National policies stressed the importance of active citizenship and social capital (NESC 2003; Taskforce on Active Citizenship 2007). Since 2008 economic recession in Ireland resulted in interventions by the European Union, the European Central Bank and the International Monetary Fund from November 2010 thus reinforcing existing fiscal constraints of local government.

ABCD was introduced as a concept for DCC through a public-private partnership. The introduction of ABCD to DCC was facilitated through developing new, and utilising established, informal relationships so that influential individuals at the helm of DCC were

---

[8] Devised by the author as an attempt to visualise the complexities concerning the application of the ABCD model and corresponding power relationships.

41

convinced to promote ABCD. It was first presented at a one-day conference at the National College of Ireland (NCI) in Dublin on 7 June 2005. Professor John L. McKnight, a founding father of ABCD, spoke at the event, which was organised by Nurture Development Limited (NDL), a private consultancy firm, in association with the NCI. This was followed by a visit by Professor Robert Putnam in 2005 and a report fostering social capital and active citizenship *Bowling Together in the Capital* (Communities First Taskforce 2007: 11). This shift was further facilitated by a change in leadership in both DCC and the Dublin City Development Board (CDB).[9] In March 2007, NDL held a second conference where McKnight and NDL were instrumental in influencing the development and adoption of ABCD as the concept underpinning DCC's community development agenda in the *Community and Neighbourhood Development Strategy 2008-2012,* which was launched on 11th December 2008. NDL played a central role in planning and drafting the Strategy and the promotion of ABCD in Dublin.[10]

A review of the Strategy and its conceptual foundations

The overarching goal of DCC's Strategy is:

> *To strengthen civil society by enhancing the connections between citizens, neighbourhoods and Dublin City Council (DCC) so that all*

---

9   The Dublin City Development Board is one of 34 CDBs that were established on the basis of the Local Government Act 2001. CDBs consist of local government, statutory agencies, local development organisations and the social partners and is tasked to encourage better coordination of efforts among members to foster economic, social and cultural development. The Dublin CDB has a social inclusion remit and works closely together with DCC's Community Development Department.

10   A workshop on ABCD took place on 28th May 2009, which was organised by Nurture Development Limited and the Futures Academy (associated with the Faculty of the Built Environment at the Dublin Institute of Technology). John McKnight was the keynote speaker. Following the workshop, an excerpt of a speech by Michelle Obama, wife of US President Barrack Obama was circulated to participants of the seminar (e.g. Lecturers of Dublin Institute of Technology, DCC, the Dublin City Development Board, and professionals from community-based organisations) by the managing director of NDL as a means to re-emphasise the value of ABCD as a leading concept for the community development work in Dublin. In her speech Ms Obama, whose husband had been working as a community organiser in Chicago, highlighted the benefits of ABCD and the positive influence of ABCD and John McKnight on her work (Obama, 16/06/2009).

will have greater and more meaningful opportunities to engage as co-producers of vibrant, sustainable communities (DCC 2008: 5).

The conceptual framework is based on four core principles, strongly influenced by Robert Putnam's (1993) concept of social capital, it draws on *Asset-Based Community Development (ABCD), Active Citizenship, Participatory Democracy* and *Social Inclusion* albeit that each of these principles in loosely defined (*ibid*: 3-4). ABCD stresses the pivotal role of elevating local areas through the identification and mobilisation of accessible local resources or assets by local people whilst being cognisant of wider structural developments within which local areas are embedded (McKnight 1996; McKnight and Kretzmann 1986). The Strategy in Dublin, however, describes ABCD as an overly inward-looking concept: it fails to reference underlying structural reasons for inequality and disparities and their adverse impact on the capacity to access and mobilise indigenous social capital and resources. *Active Citizenship* is portrayed as a non-conflictual style of interaction between citizens and the state. The Strategy uncritically stresses the enabling role the local authority plays in facilitating citizens to "engage in a participatory fashion in self-government" (DCC 2008: 4). *Participatory Democracy* is described as a process that helps build the capacity of people to address issues of concern locally and harness structured input from local areas to inform and facilitate corresponding to existing DCC decision-making processes in particular Local Area Committees (LACs), a local authority structure with little political and executive powers. In the context of power, empowerment and active citizenship, Cronin (2009: 65) stresses the need for a greater horizontal relationship between public service providers and citizens but concludes a prior need to reform existing political culture and power relations. *Social Inclusion* is described as the integration of socially excluded individuals into existing local networks and groups within the neighbourhoods they live in. There is no acknowledgement that social inclusion is a complex and ideologically laden concept that revolves around changing power relationships structural reasons for exclusion. No reference is made to whether the four key concepts complement one another to achieve the Strategy's objectives. Community development is an elastic concept and it is not clear how the principles relate to DCC's understanding of community development which is itself derived from the European Community's Development Policy.

Community development policy is grounded on the principle of sustainable, equitable and participatory human and social development. Promotion of human rights, democracy, the rule of law and good governance are an integral part of it. The main objective of Community development must be to reduce and, eventually, to eradicate poverty (DCC 2008: 8).

The implementation process

The examination below of the two pilot approaches in two neighbourhoods (covering the period from November 2008 until mid-2011), illustrates the implementation of the ABCD-informed Strategy. First, however, some core implementation tools are outlined.

Neighbourhood Grant Schemes are a core implementation strategy for ABCD. The importance of nurturing a sense of ownership of public space among local people is emphasised as a crucial goal of ABCD. DCC's strategy encourages responsible citizens to engage in a DCC-assisted beautification of their neighbourhood through the development of community gardens, the organisation of local festivals, and measures directed at upgrading public (meeting) places. The Strategy proposes establishment of two neighbourhood grant schemes with a view to stimulating community action, which mirrors ABCD practice in the United States (Green *et al.* 2006). The *Neighbourhood Matching Grants Scheme* encourages informal voluntary organisations to address the physical improvement of 'their' neighbourhood, funding received could be matched financially or by in-kind contributions. The *Active Citizenship Mini Grants Scheme* provides an allocation of seed funding for a small number of individuals to initiate "a practical neighbourhood enhancement initiative" and provide small capital grants for local people to take on a *practical* neighbourhood enhancement initiative. The Strategy proposes that local neighbourhood fora "or local residents association in conjunction with the City Council" assess funding applications. It also recommends the formation of an internal *Neighbourhood Revitalisation Unit* to manage the process and that DCC community development section should play a brokerage role in supporting *viable* ideas and to work with other groups to identify local sponsors such as "Credit Unions, Area Based Partnerships and Family Resource Centres etc. to assist such local groups in managing money and making reports" (DCC 2008: 8).

A core part of the strategy is its focus on complementing the work of others (DCC 2008: 5). It acknowledges the experience and knowledge of a variety of state-funded special purpose organisations such as Area(-based) Partnership Companies, Community Development Projects, Family Resource Centres and Youth organisations and stresses the importance of forging strategic alliances involving relevant special purpose organisations "in an effort to add value to *our* [i.e. DCC's] respective services/supports" (DCC 2008: 10, emphasis added). It is unclear how such intentions have been discussed with and communicated to relevant agencies by the DCB (the lead agency for local/community development in Dublin City) or were formally conveyed to stakeholders through alternative channels. The two state-funded Area Partnership Companies that operate in the two pilot areas were neither informed about the establishment of these pilot projects, nor invited to the launch of the Strategy.[11]

The establishment of *Neighbourhood Fora* was part of the DCC strategies city-wide neighbourhood development approach, these would be local mechanisms to feed information into a DCC-facilitated central forum and LACs. These local fora were intended to be independent and citizen-centred, non-political and non sectarian (DCC 2008: 11). The connection between these fora and LACs should facilitate the transfer of relevant information into the political sphere thus strengthening local democracy and increase the potential for achieving positive local change especially by functioning as a link between DCC and local people, communicating needs that cannot be satisfied by the mobilisation of local assets and facilitating a better tailored delivery of services by DCC.

Piloting the Strategy: Learning from local experience

The ABCD-informed neighbourhood revitalisation process was tested in two pilot areas Clongriffin and Drimnagh (Figure 2). The designation of two pilot areas that differ considerably in urban structure, demographic and socio-economic composition was deliberate to ascertain how ABCD would work in different neighbourhoods. Clongriffin is an unfinished new town on Dublin's Northern Fringe, located about 10 kilometres north of the city centre, adjoining the northern city suburb of Donaghmede. It is part of a larger

---

[11]   Northside Partnership in Clongriffin and KWCD Partnership in Drimnagh.

mixed-use development with a planned population of 35,000-40,000 in individual family houses, terraced houses, multi-storey apartment blocks and with retail space. The 2008 crisis meant the overall development remains uncompleted and most retail units are still vacant. A new commuter town with few local jobs, it caters for young urban professionals and young families and has a high share of 'transient population' (including foreign nationals) in temporary rented accommodation. Drimnagh is a low-rise, low-density inner suburb built in the 1930s located south of the inner city containing over 1,200 houses and considered disadvantaged, with parts of it being ranked very disadvantaged. The area is a settled area that has an active and vibrant community and voluntary sector.

Figure 2: Location of the two ABCD pilot areas

Map 1: Drimnagh (Blue Boundary)   Map 2: Clongriffin (Red Boundary)

Map 3: Dublin City

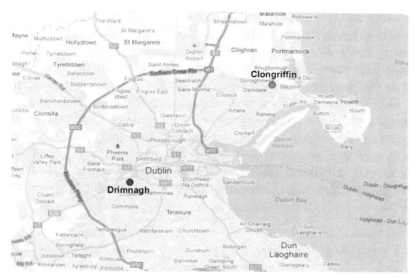

Sources: Dublin City Development Board / Pobal (Maps 1 and 2) and Google maps (Map 3)

As discussed earlier ABCD was first introduced to DCC staff in 2007. Thirteen staff underwent a short ABCD NDL training course which covered the basic toolkit and techniques that underscore the ABCD model (Russell 2007). This included community organising or mobilisation of local volunteers as catalysts for the identification of local assets as the basis for bottom-up community action. Training included 'door-to-door learning conversations' as a central method for approaching residents and eliciting useful information on motivations of people (DCC 2008: 7). Staff had mixed views regarding the quality and depth of the training provided and the role ABCD could play in assisting their local work. Some saw the language and methods as "too American" and were concerned regarding their potential to communicate to, engage with and get buy in from local people. Others were more positive. Some saw similarities with DCC's face-to-face community development model as practiced in the 1970s and so questioned the novelty of ABCD.

In September 2008, DCC allocated three staff members in each area for a number of days per week to establish links within the two pilot communities and build rapport by targeting "key people and existing formal and informal voluntary organisations". Ultimately, the stated aim is to connect citizens with a similar interest who are supported to develop and pursue actions contributing to the betterment of the neighbourhood. Context was important. The government announced budget cutbacks in October 2008 and a staff member expressed that "especially in these times, with limited public resources, it is important for us that people do things and help themselves".

Staff in Drimnagh, where engaging with local residents was reported to be less problematic than in Clongriffin, had a much more positive experience in, and outlook on, implementing ABCD than their colleagues in Clongriffin. So far, the pilots showed that Drimnagh, a place with a history, common memories and a mixed age profile, provides a much less challenging platform for launching ABCD than the new town of Clongriffin where, according to an interviewee:

> *The basics just were not there. For ABCD, the basics need to be there. Physical stuff. The shops, the Luas [Dublin's light rail system], the buses and so on. Clongriffin did not have that. People were concerned about these basics. There was the issue with 'pyrite' and many people were living in half-empty apartment blocks. So for ABCD to happen, other developments have to happen first.*

To a varying degree, the pilots showed levels of civic engagement could be increased and connections between people with similar interests could be fostered. Other aims and objectives, however, have not been progressed considerably. At the time of the research, the process of developing operational neighbourhood fora was still at a conceptual level. Also, the rolling out of the two small grants schemes had not happened. There was no implementation of an "annual collation of success stories" or development of "empirically sound evaluation tools to measure social capital and quality of life trends within pilot areas' (DCC 2008: 9). Up to 2011 DCC staff were unaware about the extent to which empirically robust evaluation tools have been developed. Furthermore, existing interaction with other relevant state-funded local development bodies remains *ad hoc* and informal, rather than being regarded operational at strategic level as originally anticipated in the Strategy.

Analysis

To date, ABCD has not been utilised as a means to form an enabling model encouraging the formation of strong local associations or fora in the city of Dublin that could possibly exert political influence or demand support around issues that cannot be simply addressed by mobilising, bundling and utilising local assets. Rather the ABCD-informed Strategy has a number of weaknesses, which jeopardise the potential of citizens to become key drivers to identify, unleash and harness indigenous assets and the potentiality of 'their' neighbourhood. The main four weaknesses are discussed below:

- Efforts to mobilise residents in the pilot areas were not paralleled by a corresponding development of intended structures and support mechanisms (neighbourhood fora and neighbourhood revitalisation units);
- The Strategy stresses the important role of other agencies that offer local knowledge and know-how but there is little evidence this objective was pursued. Rather the strategy appears to duplicate and compete with work of state-funded local development companies;
- The recent contraction of the economy led to a significant reduction in funding for state-funded local development initiatives. In this light, ABCD's focus on citizens as key drivers to increase the potentiality of 'their' neighbourhood runs the danger of the Strategy pushing neighbourhoods to ensure all place-based resources are fully utilised by local actors before support from the state/city hall should be considered. It is difficult to comprehend how the DCC Strategy, by focusing on the mobilisation of local skills and 'assets' by people affected by poverty, could make a meaningful contribution to the betterment of poor areas. If deployed based on this interpretation of self-help, the adopted Strategy effectively promotes an *inverse-care law,* whereby those neighbourhoods 'who already-have' receive and those 'who have-not' get less or are ignored (Figure 1, Mode 2);
- At a conceptual level responsibility for addressing local manifestations of structural disadvantage is shifted from the political and administrative spheres into the realm of civil society. The process can be used to *exert managerial control* (Figure 1, Mode 3).

The Strategy conforms to a market-driven agenda that underpins the re-alignment of state-funded local/community development agencies and national efforts directed at promoting active citizenship and volunteering (Taskforce on Active Citizenship 2007). It does not address the role, and continuing adverse effects, of previous planning and ongoing housing policies or other structural forces on shaping communities and community well-being. Empowerment and active citizenship is limited to addressing issues *within and via* the institutional and political framework provided by the local authority. This has to be understood in the context of the clientelist nature of the Irish political system coupled with the subordinate role elected local politicians play vis-à-vis unelected local government officials (Komito 1993; Ó Broin and Waters 2007; Hughes 2007). This is a systemic barrier to achieving local empowerment (a cornerstone of the Strategy). Under the model suggested in the Strategy, potential dissent can be institutionalised within local government structures whose own piecemeal planning policies have been responsible for many challenges now faced by local communities (Bartley and Waddington 2001).

Conclusion

An analysis of DCC's ABCD-led approach has to take into consideration the structural forces that influence levels of poverty and affluence in neighbourhoods. These issues concern political sponsorship, intent and empowerment, the conceptual alignment of actions with the original ABCD approach and the role of other statutory, state-funded agencies and voluntary organisations with a social inclusion agenda.

In Dublin, the introduction of ABCD was a result of a co-operation between a private company, NDL, and senior key individuals of DCC who could be convinced of the merits of ABCD as a new model for promoting community development in the city. The potential for empowerment of people provided by the Strategy in Dublin, however, seems to be ring-fenced and limited to opportunities provided within the local authority-led institutional and political framework. This stretches the concept of ABCD as an instrument to empower citizens, (the core of ABCD philosophy), beyond recognition. The role of relevant external agencies and other statutory bodies has not been sufficiently explored. The analysis suggests that the ABCD-informed community and neighbourhood development approach in Dublin is organised and implemented in a top-down, rather than bottom up, way. The principle of empowerment appears to be reduced to the (re)presentation of local issues within narrow institutional limits provided by the formal policy framework of DCC.

ABCD as presently conceived and implemented fails to address the lack of connection between politics and governance structures. The people in Ireland have expectations of other initiatives that seek new creative ways to involve citizens at the local level in public decision-making (see Chapter 3). President Michael D. Higgins, in his inaugural speech, calls for a "transition in institutions, building on many positive initiatives under way in communities" and supporting the most excluded to participate in society and all citizens "to make their own imaginative and practical contribution to the shaping of our shared future" (Irish Times 2011). Under the DCC-controlled governance system in Dublin, where unelected officials have significantly greater executive decision-making power than elected politicians, ABCD is a neighbourhood revitalisation model that assists the local authority in achieving its objectives rather than as an enabling instrument fostering the empowerment of communities (Figure 1 Mode 1). It fails to meet its aspiration for genuine development of a new, citizen-led model of community participation in decision-making.

The concept of ABCD is relatively new in the Irish context and has not been tested over a prolonged period of time. The approach has merit if adapted to reflect the local context. Wider economic and structural aspects impact on neighbourhoods and influence how local communities can influence decision-making processes on issues affecting their area. If applied according to its ethos and resourced with a compatible support structure, ABCD could possibly make a positive contribution to locally addressing negative effects of the economic downturn and other forces adversely impacting on communities in Dublin.

CHAPTER 6
FROM TALK TO IMPACT: ASSESSING THE CONSULTATION AND PARTICIPATION OF PEOPLE EXPERIENCING POVERTY IN POLICY DEVELOPMENT

Paul Ginnell

There is no point in a Government body saying they are going to do this or that unless they sit down with the people who are actually using the service to understand exactly what is going on on the ground (Irish delegate to the EU Meeting of People Experiencing Poverty 2009).

Introduction

This paper looks at the issue of participation in the context of the EU social inclusion strategy, the social Open Method of Cooperation (OMC), and asks what the impact has been of the voices of people experiencing poverty and their organisations on policy development in Ireland and how can they can be strengthened. The article also looks briefly at examples from other EU Member States to see if lessons can be drawn for Ireland.[12]

Participation of citizens in decisions that affect their lives is widely accepted as an essential element of good governance and as a right. It has a number of benefits. Firstly, it benefits society in terms of the quality of decisions that get made. It also benefits those who take part through increasing their self-esteem by being valued for the contribution they make and a sense of having some control over aspects of their lives (Richardson 1983 and Burton 2007). Participative democracy, which involves the ongoing direct engagement of citizens in decision making and recognises the essential role of civil society organisations in building the capacity of citizens, complements formal representative democracy.

Participative democracy plays a particularly important role in recognising the disengagement from decision making of many people from disadvantaged communities where the majority have no

---

[12] This paper is a development of the chapter by the same title by Paul Ginnell and Michael Mackey which was published in *Ireland and the EU Social Inclusion Strategy: Lessons learned and the road ahead* by EAPN Ireland in 2010.

connection in general with those with responsibility for the policies that impact on their lives.

Participation takes place across a range of levels, from information through consultation, to co-decision making and other levels and forms in between (Combat Poverty Agency 2006). The quality of participation at each level is important in itself and each builds on the previous stage.

For participation to be effective there must be openness to engagement from those with responsibility for policy making, backed up by commitment to ensuring that it is effective in influencing policy and properly resourced and facilitated.

The EU Social Inclusion Strategy

This EU Social Inclusion Strategy, which is the context of this paper, was an important development at EU level which began in 2000. The Amsterdam Treaty in 1997 was significant in a number of ways including allowing for such a strategy. First of all it gave the EU a role in relation to addressing social exclusion (Articles 136 and 137). Secondly, it provided the basis at EU level through which the EU could coordinate a process, whereby Member States could work together to achieve agreed goals on policy areas where the EU did not have a remit or competence to pass binding legislation. This process is called the Open Method of Coordination (OMC). Through the OMC the European Commission works with Member States to agree on common objectives and then coordinates a reporting process whereby Member States send their plans and progress reports to the Commission who publishes their own annual reports on progress towards the common objectives. These reports contain an EU overview as well as short reports on each Member State and the Member States reports can also make recommendations on specific policy areas. This process started with a focus on employment in 1998 and then in 2000 expanded to the area of poverty and social exclusion with the first plans being submitted to the European Commission in 2001. The agreed overall aim of the OMC on poverty and social inclusion was "to make a decisive impact on poverty by 2010" (European Council 2000: 1).

Policy Overview on Participation

The next section of the paper gives an overview of the EU and national policy context for enhancing the participation of people experiencing poverty and social exclusion and their organisations in policy making.

<u>EU level</u>
The European Union has progressively addressed the issue of participation over time. Social dialogue, which promotes engagement in the employment area between employers and employees, as well as in the social area with stakeholders including NGOs, is a key approach at EU level.

Between 1974 and 1994 the EU introduced three Poverty Programmes, which allowed for actions in Member States and on a transnational basis, to identify innovative ways of tackling poverty. A key aspect of these Programmes was the focus on the participation of "poor people" themselves in actions to address poverty. The third Poverty Programme, Poverty 3, also included a focus on developing partnership as an approach in tackling poverty. Lessons from the Poverty Programmes had an impact on the development of the community sector in Ireland, particularly in the direct engagement of people experiencing poverty and their organisations in policy making. These Programmes helped set the foundations for a greater focus on participation in the EU social inclusion strategy.

In 2001, the European Commission set out a clear strategy for participation when they produced 'European Governance – A White Paper' which states that:

> *The quality, relevance and effectiveness of EU policies depends on ensuring wide participation throughout the policy chain – from conception to implementation. Improved participation is likely to create more confidence in the end result and in the institutions which deliver policies. Participation crucially depends on central governments following an inclusive approach when developing and implementing polices (European Commission 2001: 17).*

The Lisbon Treaty Article 8B also attempts to address the democratic deficit through the 'citizens initiative' where one million citizens can put a policy proposal on the agenda of the European Commission. It also commits the EU to consultations on policy development and to open, transparent and regular dialogue with citizens and representative associations (European Union 2007: 15).

Over the past ten years of the EU Open Method of Coordination (OMC) for Social Inclusion, participation has been a core objective. This began with the Common Objectives adopted in Nice in 2000 and continued with the revised Common Objectives for Social Protection and Social Inclusion in 2006, which includes the clear overall objective of "Good governance, transparency and the involvement of stakeholders in the design, implementation and monitoring of policy" (European Commission 2006a: 2). Among the three specific objectives on social inclusion is:

> that social inclusion policies are well coordinated and involve all levels of government and relevant actors, including people experiencing poverty, that they are efficient and effective and mainstreamed into all relevant public policies, including economic, budgetary, education and training policies and Structural Fund (notably ESF) Programmes (European Commission 2006a: 4).

The reference to all stages of policy development and the specific mention of people experiencing poverty is significant and provides a basis for a focus on these issues throughout the 10 years of the social inclusion process up to 2010.

The annual EU Meetings of People Experiencing Poverty[13] are a part of the EU's social inclusion strategy and provide an opportunity for people experiencing poverty to participate directly at EU level in the process.

The current round of OMC on social inclusion came to an end in 2010 and the EU has been fine-tuning its strategy for the current ten-year period. This began with the publication in 2010 of *Europe 2020: A strategy for smart, sustainable and inclusive growth*. Europe 2020 includes, for the first time, a poverty reduction target which has now been agreed as "to lift 20 million people out of poverty and social exclusion by 2020" (European Commission 2010b: 32). It also includes a European Flagship Against Poverty, which is the key initiative that addresses how the poverty target is to be achieved. The strategy also poses challenges for strengthening participation over the next ten years and

---

[13] The annual Meetings of People Experiencing Poverty are an EU Presidency event which began in 2001. They are an important part of the social inclusion strategy at EU level and also complement actions taken at Member State level. At EU level the EAPN is responsible for coordinating this process with EAPN national networks having responsibility for supporting the delegations to prepare and take part. For Information on the Meetings of People Experiencing Poverty see EAPN Ireland webpage www.eapn.ie/eapn/participation/people-experiencing-poverty .

building on past lessons and practice. While full details of the Platform will not be agreed until the end of 2011, it is now less clear how the participation of people experiencing poverty and their organisations, particularly at a grass roots level, is to be structured within the next ten years so that they can have and will have an influence over policy development.

National level

Consultation and participative processes are not new in Ireland. The participation of people experiencing poverty and social exclusion and their organisations in decision-making was a principle of the National Anti-Poverty Strategy (NAPS) in 1997 and the *White Paper on a Framework for Supporting Voluntary Activity and for Developing the Relationship between the State and the Community and Voluntary Sector* in 2000 included Active Citizenship as a key principle and defined it as "the active role of people, communities and voluntary organisations in decision-making which directly affects them. This extends the concept of formal citizenship and democratic society from one of basic civil, political and social and economic rights to one of direct democratic participation and responsibility' (Government of Ireland 2000: 14).

Since 1996 community and voluntary organisations have also had a separate pillar in national social partnership, including a role in overseeing implementation of the Government's social inclusion commitments in the social partnership agreements. The role of the Community and Voluntary Pillar is recognised by the European Commission in its reports on Ireland's engagement with the process (European Commission 2007c).

Participation is also an element of engagement in decision making at local level particularly in the context of the County and City Development Boards, the Strategic Policy Committees in local authorities and the RAPID programme.[14]

The existence of these structures is important and complements, but is not a substitute for, the direct participation of people experiencing

[14] The Revitalising Areas by Planning, Investment and Development (RAPID) programme is aimed at improving the quality of life and the opportunity available to residents of the most disadvantaged communities in Irish cities and towns. It aims, in a focused and practical way, to reduce the deprivations faced by residents of disadvantaged communities. It attempts to do this through targeting significant state resources at the needs of disadvantaged areas.

poverty and social exclusion and their organisations. The Community Platform, a network of 30 national anti-poverty and equality networks and a member of the Community and Voluntary Pillar, plays an important role in bringing the voice of these people to social partnership and the wider policy development process.

A strong community infrastructure in Ireland is critical to supporting good participation. The Irish Government's support for the community infrastructure has been a positive example in the EU. The report from the EU Peer Review[15] of the Irish Social Inclusion Forum highlighted this support as an essential precondition for the Social Inclusion Forum[16] and an example of good practice to other Member States (Swinnen 2007). This has also been highlighted in other reports on the OMC (EAPN 2003: 15; Combat Poverty Agency 2006). Ongoing support for community organisations at national and local levels is essential to achieving the governance objective of the OMC inclusion.

However, the current approach of Government to cut its funding for community development organisations, including the discontinuation of the Community Development Programme as the formerly independent organisations are 'integrated' into the Local and Community Development Programme, undermines the process of supporting the participation of people experiencing poverty and their organisations in policy making. These developments indicate a change in approach by the Irish Government and sends out a negative message to other Member States.

The Irish Government alongside the Combat Poverty Agency and the NGOs in the Irish National Anti-Poverty Networks were partners in an EU transnational project in 2000, which were involved in the

---

[15] Peer Reviews are an element of the EU Open Method of Coordination. The aim is to bring a number of Member States together to analyse a good practice example of policy or practice highlighted by one Member State and draw on their own experience and to highlight learning that could be transferable to other Member States.

[16] The National Social Inclusion Forum was coordinated until 2009 by the National Economic and Social Forum. It is the only formal opportunity for people experiencing poverty and social exclusion and their organisations to engage directly with policy makers on the design and implementation of social inclusion policy. Specifically the SIF provides an opportunity for those involved to input their views on key policies and implementation issues and participate in the monitoring and evaluation of social inclusion plans as well as offer advice on any shortcomings. Depending on the timing of the SIF it also has the objective of contributing to the process of drawing up Ireland's Plans and Reports to the EU OMC process as was the case for the second NAPincl 2003-2005 and the first NSSPSI 2006-2008. Six fora were carried out between 2003 and 2009.

development of *Guidelines for Effective Involvement* (Combat Poverty Agency 2000). The Guidelines highlight that in order to support meaningful participation the purpose of the involvement needs to be clear; the way it is organised effective and that the practical issues and barriers that can make it possible or not must be addressed. These Guidelines could be revisited as a starting point for developing a much stronger, consistent and structured approach to the participation of people experiencing poverty in decision making in Ireland.

The Impact of the OMC on Participation in Ireland

Member States have to report to the European Commission on participation in the social inclusion process. This in itself helps raise the importance of participation in policy development at national level. Alongside the Commission's reports, the engagement of national and European NGOs in providing an alternative view through shadow reports or other forms of engagement, allows us to identify the quality of this participation in consultation and the wider policy making process.

Consultation and the OMC

Over the ten years since 2000 the quality of the consultation process for the development of Ireland's EU National Action Plans for Social Inclusion (NAP Inclusion) has varied greatly.

The Irish NAP Inclusion Plans from 2001-2005 and the Social Inclusion chapter of the National Reports on Strategies for Social Protection and Social Inclusion (NSSPSI)[17] in the revised process from 2006 provide a description of the consultation process. The NAP Inclusion 2001-2003 outlines the process as involving a consideration of submissions from the community and voluntary sector and Government Departments and a Round Table discussion on the integration of equality and poverty perspectives in the NAP Inclusion at the request of the Community and Voluntary Sector. It also

---

[17] From 2000-2005 Member States submitted bi-annual National Action Plans Against Poverty and Social Exclusion (National Action Plans for Social Inclusion or NAPincl for short). In 2006 following a review of the Lisbon Strategy the NAPincl became one chapter in the bi-annual National Reports on Strategies for Social Protection and Social Inclusion which also included chapters on Pensions and on Health and Long-term Care. In 2007 the Irish Government also produced a separate National Action Plan for Social Inclusion 2007-2016.

highlights that this process coincided with and was informed by the review of Ireland's National Anti-Poverty Strategy (NAPS) 1997-2007.

The NAP Inclusion 2003-2005 and the NSSPSI 2006-2008 noted the detailed consultation that took place including the publication of specific reports in each case on the consultation process. The NSSPSI 2008-2010, however, outlines reasons why a specific consultation was not necessary mainly highlighting the fact that there was a thorough process two years previously and that Ireland had a 10 year National Action Plan for Social Inclusion 2007-2016, which replaced the NAPS.

The shadow reporting process by NGOs including EAPN over the years however provides an alternative view from the experience of organisations and people on the ground and a critique of the consultation process for each of these periods.

The EAPN assessment of the consultation process for the NAP Inclusion 2001-2003 in Ireland is not positive. It states that "there was no opportunity for people affected by the Plan to input seriously to the process, due to the short timescale" (EAPN 2003: 3). It also highlighted that 'Ways of developing processes to involve people more in decisions which affect their lives need to be explored for the next review leading up to the new NAPincl in 2003" (EAPN 2003: 4).

However, there is a recognition that the lack of proper consultation for the first NAP Inclusion was improved for the 2003-2005 and 2006-2008 plans. A report on the 2003-2005 process carried out by the Community Platform and EAPN Ireland states that "the consultation on the Plan, organised by the Office for Social Inclusion and the Combat Poverty Agency, and before this by the NESF, was far reaching, thorough and well-designed and can serve as an example of good practice for this type of consultation" (EAPN Ireland and Community Platform 2005). The positive developments include the first Social Inclusion Forum.

The continuation of this positive approach to the 2006-2008 period was also commented on by the European Commission which stated in 2007 that Ireland "continues to demonstrate a clear commitment to wide-ranging consultation in the preparation of its inclusion strategy" (European Commission 2007c: 52).

However, this positive development was reversed for the 2008-2010 period when no consultation was carried out highlighting the inconsistencies and lack of overall commitment to high quality participation of people experiencing poverty and their organisations in the process.

This inconsistency on consultation on the social inclusion process is reflected in other policy areas in Ireland. A positive approach has been put in place to consult communities on how primary health care teams can better meet the needs of communities. Time will tell in terms of the outcomes from this process. A major example of a negative process has been that carried out by the Centre for Effective Services on the Community Development Programme and the Local Development Social Inclusion Programme resulting in their 'integration'. Community organisations and the Community Development Projects (CDPs) themselves have publicly commented on the flawed nature of this process, which effectively results in the closure of approximately 190 local community led organisations and on the capacity of marginalised communities and groups to participate in decisions that affect their lives.

Role of the European Commission

The Commission's role in coordinating the EU social OMC process is an essential element of the process. In order to bring greater clarity to the responsibilities of Member States, the European Commission issued a Guidance Note on the development of the National Reports in 2008. This Note emphasised the importance of strengthening the governance of the OMC and ongoing structured dialogue with all stakeholders including NGOs and people experiencing poverty at all stages of the process. However, in developing the NSSPSI 2008-2010 the Government ignored the Commission's Guidance Note (European Commission 2008) and its own good practice for the previous two periods and decided that consultation was not necessary. This lack of consultation was criticised by anti-poverty organisations and was reflected in the EAPN Ireland Shadow Report (EAPN Ireland 2008). EAPN highlighted its concerns directly to the European Commission.

The criticism of the consultation process was referred to by the European Commission in its Joint Report on Social Protection and Social Inclusion in 2009 which stated that "... the decision not to engage in a separate consultation process in advance of this NSR received some adverse publicity in Ireland" (European Commission 2009: 273).

Considering its position on governance in the OMC, this reaction from the European Commission was weak and had little impact. This highlights an overall weakness in the role of the European Commission in relation to the OMC process in that if a Member State engages positively with the process then progress can be made, but if a Member State is less positive then the Commission may highlight the issue but does not have the teeth to bring about a more positive engagement.

Conditions for Participation

The importance of proper conditions to support participation of people experiencing poverty has been raised repeatedly in relation to the OMC and involves constant learning.

In 2003, while highlighting the positive engagement in the initial phase of the consultation for the NAP Inclusion 2003-2005, the Community Platform and the EAPN Ireland report on the process also identifies that "people in poverty were not directly consulted in the preparation of the Plan. Although there was an opportunity to participate in public consultations, the language and structure of these was not specifically designed to encourage their participation" (2003: 10).

The report highlighted that there was a responsibility both on NGOs and the Government to make sure that people affected by the issues should be involved in the design, implementation and evaluation of strategies and that the proper conditions needed to be created for this to happen.

The Social Inclusion Forum is an important part in the social inclusion process in Ireland. The focus on participation in the EU social inclusion process brings greater impetus to the direct participation of people experiencing poverty and social exclusion in the Forum. Participants in their evaluation of the Social Inclusion Forum have highlighted some areas where the Forum could be strengthened to support better conditions for good participation. A number of areas were also highlighted by the EU Peer Review on the Social Inclusion Forum in 2007, which states that there was a need for sufficient resources to support the participation of stakeholders in policy development and implementation. The Peer Review report specifically highlights a number of other practical issues that need to be thought of when planning events which impact on participation. These include the type of language that is used, the timing of events, capacity building with participants to ensure they are able to fully participate and ensuring that the financial barriers are addressed including travel, childcare etc (Swinnen 2007).

The report outlines the importance of resources given by government agencies to NGOs, such as the Community Platform and EAPN Ireland to carry out preparatory meetings and focus groups and the process which began in 2007 of providing direct support for approximately 20 people experiencing poverty to participate in the meetings. Even though the Social Inclusion Forum was highlighted as an example of good practice on participation, for other Member States improvements were still needed to create the conditions for good participation.

Impact of Consultation

The other issue which is raised is the impact of initial consultation, however positive in how it is carried out, on the content of the social inclusion plans and their implementation. While highlighting the positive elements of the early stages of the consultation process for the 2003-2005 NAPincl, the Community Platform and EAPN report also states that "the impact on the content of the Plan is less obvious" and that the process "would appear to have very little impact on actual Government policy and have diluted Government responsibility and accountability by creating an impression of broad agreement when, in fact, the views of anti-poverty constituencies are hardly reflected at all". It warns against the danger of this lack of impact resulting in "consultation fatigue" (2005: 5).

In 2007 the European Commission raised the general point for Ireland and other Member States where the drafting process was open, that "in all Member States there is scope for improving the quality of this involvement, ensuring that it actually impacts on policies and priorities" (European Commission 2007b: 59). For Ireland it specifically mentions that "the direct involvement of stakeholders is more limited in the area of implementation, monitoring and evaluation" (European Commission 2007c: 65). This report also emphasised the need to address the 'implementation gap' in existing legislation, policy programmes and taskforce recommendations. These concerns had also been raised in previous Joint Reports (European Commission 2003: 73).

The concern over implementation is also raised in relation to the impact of the Social Inclusion Forum. Evaluations from SIF participants, over the years have highlighted that this is an ongoing concern for many. Comments by participants include the need for "clearer feedback on issues brought up in past Fora and where they ended up" (NESF 2008: 138) and that "Themes should focus on why recommendations are not in place or not working" (NESF 2007: 124). The EU Peer Review report in 2007 also highlighted that an essential part of consultation is that authorities must listen to opinions and views of other stakeholders and that they are clear on the outcomes and impact of such consultation. It also highlighted that public authorities must not only listen to actors but give systematic feedback and discuss what happened to their advice (Swinnen 2007: 20). The need for ongoing evaluation and monitoring of the impact of participation processes such as the Social Inclusion Forum is also highlighted by the Peer Review (Swinnen 2007: 26).

While Irish delegates' evaluations of the EU Meetings of People Experiencing Poverty are generally positive in terms of the opportunity to participate, a recurring issue for them is the need to know if these meetings are having any impact either at EU or national level. As one delegate stated "I really hope that the crossover of information that I saw in Brussels will have some effect and I do hope it will continue". Recent meetings have been structured to begin to address this issue through the preparation of delegates, engagement with policy makers from Member States and EU institutions and direct feedback at the meetings themselves.

The lack of follow through from initial consultation, to how this is reflected in the plans and their implementation, undermines the process and its sustainability. It is crucial that those experiencing poverty and social exclusion and their organisations are convinced that their participation is valued and has an impact on policy and its implementation. Participants need to see the impact of their contribution or at least receive feedback on what has been taken on board, what has not and why.

This chapter has shown that the participation of people experiencing poverty and their organisations in Ireland's engagement in the OMC process is mainly at the level of consultation. At national level the Community and Voluntary Pillar is involved in meetings with Departments on the implementation of aspects of the OMC which are included as part of social partnership processes. While this engagement is important, it is essential to assess the impact of this process past the consultation phase. Greater efforts need to be made to identify how participation can move beyond the initial stage to a level which has greater influence over policy development and implementation.

Learning from other Member States

A range of reports highlight positive examples of consultation and wider participation including the European Commission's Joint Reports, and the EAPN annual reports on the implementation of the OMC inclusion. The Mainstreaming Social Inclusion EU Transnational project final report (Combat Poverty Agency 2006) also highlights a number of examples of participation at different stages of the policy making process from Member States including Ireland, Portugal, Czech Republic, France, Norway and Northern Ireland. Many of these indicate elements of good practice without the existence of a broad strategic approach for developing participation within the Member States.

In some regions standards and more formal structure for representative democracy are more progressed. Belgium has a Participation Decree adopted in legislation which supports participation in policy making. However, in Scotland, the process, while not on a legislative basis, is more progressed and deep rooted at administrative level.

In 2005 the Scottish Executive adopted *National Standards for Community Engagement*. These standards set out best practice guidelines for engagement between communities and public agencies and are structured as a way of implementing the Community Planning obligation in the Local Government Scotland Act. The standards are coordinated through the Scottish Community Development Centre (SCDC) and involve standards for a range of areas including support, planning, methods, working together, sharing information, improvement, feedback and monitoring and evaluation. Support materials have been developed including a National Standards Booklet and advice notes on areas, such as how to apply the standard in a range of different contexts including with young people, rural communities and equalities groups.

The standards have been tested and were developed after a wide process of consultation with communities and agencies.

EAPN Ireland recently completed research on effective consultation (McInerney 2011). The report looks at practice in other countries to see if any lessons can be drawn to support better practice in Ireland. The research shows that in many international studies of good practice on participation Ireland is highlighted as a positive example, particularly due to the existence of the Community and Voluntary Pillar in the social partnership process and the annual Social Inclusion Forum. However, as highlighted above, at national level there is criticism in relation to the impact and effectiveness of participation and consultation processes. The research looks at evaluations of other international examples and concludes that developing a legislative basis for consultation and participation is significant and that this must be backed up by guidelines and procedures for its implementation. This legislative basis signals to officials and public representatives that it needs to be taken seriously, but that this in itself is not sufficient to make it work. Even where there is a strong legislative or policy basis, included in the international examples outlined above, implementation is still a major issue where there is not sufficient institutional backing. Where it might be more successful is due to the interest and commitment of an individual. Therefore, a legislative or high level policy basis is not sufficient on its own but must be backed up by an institutional and system wide commitment to participation. This needs to be embedded in the system with widespread ownership of the process.

Conclusion

The common objective on Governance in the EU OMC inclusion and the requirement of Member States to report on this, brought greater focus on how people experiencing poverty and social exclusion and their organisations engaged in policy making on social inclusion at national level. The European Commission's Joint Reports repeatedly highlight shortfalls in how Member States, including Ireland, achieved this objective stressing the importance of high quality participation, which needs to be resourced and go beyond the preparation stage to implementation and evaluation (European Commission 2007). However, shortfalls by Member States are partially made possible by the weak monitoring role of the European Commission. Therefore, the resolve with which the Commission tackles bad practice needs to be strengthened alongside the enhanced capacity to bring pressure on Member States. Unfortunately, in relation to its monitoring in the social area the Commission and EU overall seem to be moving in the opposite direction with more severe forms of monitoring reserved for economic policy.

It is clear that the majority of participation in decision making in Ireland is at the level of consultation, the quality of which in itself needs to be more effective and consistent. Within this, the quality of processes to ensure the active engagement of people experiencing poverty and social exclusion and their organisations needs to be greatly strengthened. The EU Meetings of People Experiencing Poverty offer a positive example and the Social Inclusion Forum shows the potential for improving practice.

The report from the EU Peer Review of the Social Inclusion Forum in 2007 highlights some of the key elements when it concluded that "the preconditions for participation does not drop from the sky. You need to work on it. The preconditions for good participation start from having clear objectives, having resources to support the process, empowering people and ensuring feedback" (Swinnen 2007: 26).

Strong community development organisations at local and national level and the support they receive from the State are key. The decision of the Government to cease funding to the Community Development Programme is a very negative move which will impact directly on the capacity of local communities to have a collective voice. Future governments need to immediately reconsider and reverse the current policy of dismantling the independent community infrastructure which is central to supporting participative democracy in marginalised communities and therefore good governance.

Learning from other Member States, while also highlighting similar difficulties as in Ireland, also demonstrate that it is possible to be ambitious and develop and implement clear structures for meaningful participation. This states from a legislative basis, but also demands clear structures and ownership and a commitment to making it work. The benefits are better and result in more effective policies. If implemented properly people experiencing poverty and their organisations will also recognise that their contribution is respected.

The current development of a code of practice is a useful place to start and should build on existing learning including the *Guidelines for Effective Involvement* developed in 2000. It should also clearly take into account the vast amount of learning from the past. However, it then needs to ensure the code of practice is adopted at a high, even legislative, level and accepted at an administrative level as an essential element in decision making.

As the EU puts in place the final elements of the Europe 2020 Strategy, including the Platform Against Poverty which will address the future of the social OMC, it is clear that stakeholder engagement, while named, is not a core element. It is disappointing that, despite the weaknesses of the past 10 years, the EU is not building on the lessons learned but is taking a step back from encouraging and supporting better practice at EU and Member States level.

Therefore, despite the sense of disillusionment that exists among organisations representing people experiencing poverty and social exclusion it is up to them to take the initiative and continue to push for stronger and more effective structures and practice for participation in decision making. This is important now more than ever as Ireland puts in place policies to address the crisis. These policies have the potential to create greater equality across all of society, or to condemn people and marginalised communities to greater levels of poverty and social exclusion for generations to come.

CHAPTER 7
BARRIERS AND BARRICADES: EXPLORING THE CHALLENGES TO BUILDING SOCIAL MOVEMENTS FOR PEOPLE WHO ARE POOR

Mike Allen

Introduction

In this contribution I want to explore how the core themes of this series - Politics, Participation and Power - relate to people who are poor and, more specifically, to the social movements they may create or in which they seek to participate. I will draw on work concerning social movements of people who are homeless, drawing particularly on discussions at a European level (Anker 2008; Allen 2009; Paasche 2010). My own contribution to the homeless debate is largely theoretical but I will also draw more extensively from my practical involvement of working with organisations and movements of people who are unemployed. This experience comes from my period as General Secretary of the Irish National Organisation of the Unemployed (INOU), from its establishment in the late 1980s through until the end of the 1990s, but it also draws on experience with the European Network of the Unemployed (ENU) and other participant-based anti-poverty initiatives over this period (Allen 1998; Royall 2002; Linders 2007).

Throughout the chapter I will use the term 'people who are poor' as a general term to cover a variety of conditions relating both to individuals and the communities in which they live. I will develop the meaning of this term as we go along.

I want to start by referring to the framework of social partnership that Professor Gary Murphy uses in his contribution. He characterises Social Partnership essentially as an interaction of conflicting interest groups on the formation of public policy. Murphy describes how 'interest groups' in society form and seek to maximise their influence on public policy to progress their own interests and the interests of their members. Within this framework, we would expect, in any open, developed society, that groups of citizens who share a particular interest would come together to establish organisations to promote their interests. These interest groups use whatever structures or mechanisms are available in society at that time to pursue these goals. Murphy describes particular interest groups - Trade Unions, employers, farmers and, more latterly, the Community and Voluntary Sector - entering into Social Partnership as just one means of promoting their interests in competition with other conflicting interests. From this perspective, Social Partnership is just a recent addition to the traditional mechanisms of influence – lobbying, donations to politicians or political parties, seeking favourable coverage in the press, etc.

It is worth noting that this is, of course, a very limited description of Irish Social Partnership. It sets aside much of the high-minded discourse on 'collective problem solving' which was commonplace during the boom years, perhaps best captured in the title of a book published in 2007 "Saving the Future: How Social Partnership Shaped Ireland's Economic Success" (Hastings *et al.* 2007). My own sense is that this more complex and optimistic description of Social Partnership in the Irish context (O'Donnell 2000) is currently being too easily dismissed because the success has evaporated and there are elements in social partnership which we will need to revisit if we are to build a just and sustainable society.

Nevertheless, Murphy's framework of interest groups engaging in a process simply to maximise their own benefit gives a true, if arguably partial, description of the process. More specifically, it also sets a very useful framework for what I want to discuss. I will comment towards the end of the paper on how the issues I raise impact on more sophisticated and optimistic understandings of Ireland's Social Partnership experience. Professor Murphy used a typology that characterised the routes to influence as being 'markets' and 'networks'. He argued that Irish Governance is characterised as having lots of markets and lots of networks.

When it comes to influence through markets, the poor have a fairly obvious problem. They have little or no market influence. Advanced capitalism is not interested in them because they do not have the money to buy anything and very often they don't have the skills to make anything – or at least anything which would generate sufficient profit to justify the investment. Castells refers to "those who are structurally irrelevant from the perspective of the profit-making programs of global capitalism, either as workers (inadequately educated and living in areas without the proper infrastructural and institutional environment for global production) or as consumers (too poor to be part of the market), or both" (Castells 2009: 33).

New Perspectives Quarterly editor Nathan Gardels expressed it more succinctly: 'We don't need what they have and they can't buy what we want to sell.'

In theory, within a liberal pluralist version of society, groups that have low market power can compensate by maximising their 'network power' through collective action or the development of social movements. Is this what actually happens? Is it possible for marginalised groups, by virtue of creating an effective 'interest group', to redress their marginalisation? What are the problems that arise for people who are poor and the groups, if any, which attempt to promote their interest? I want to look at the ways in which people have tried to understand how social movements work and how these ideas are relevant to the particular problems faced by people who are poor. I will briefly look at the major discourses of social movements Resource Mobilisation Theory, New Social Movement theory and the work of Piven and Cloward on 'Poor People's Movements'

Resource Mobilisation Theory

The key insight of Resource Mobilisation Theory (RMT) is that effective social movements do not emerge just because of the number or extent of grievances in society at any given time, but rather because of the availability of *resources* to nourish a social movement. RMT looks at the ways in which social movement organisations (SMOs) raise resources (including money, but also influence) and deploy it to further their objectives (McCarthy and Zald 1977).

The very name of the theory points to the problems which people who are poor will face. RMT distinguishes between resources, which are derived internally and externally (Cress and Snow 1996). By definition, individuals and communities that are poor do not have sufficient internal resources to effectively mobilize. For instance, a group of people who are unemployed and attempting to form an 'unemployed interest group', may have some internal resources to call on, but these are limited and of a particular nature. Depending on their class background they may have professional expertise and may have linkages – through their former employment – to political or other networks of influence. We will look at this later. They have, probably, the resource of time. What they clearly lack is the financial resources needed to establish an organisation – money for an office, equipment, postage, banners, even a place to meet. In most interest groups such basic resources can be drawn together from the membership, but where the members are unemployed and so already below the poverty threshold.

At a very early stage in setting up their organisation, they find themselves in need of drawing in external resources. The question of whether the source of external resources influences the direction of a social movement has been debated within RMT. Two broad perspectives emerge. The 'social control hypothesis' argues that the providers of external resources moderate the goals and tactics of SMOs, ensuring that radical actions are curtailed. Others argue that it professionalises goals and tactics, making them more palatable but also more effective (Cress and Snow 1996).

At the most basic level, in Ireland organisations seeking external resources have been able to draw upon either State sources or non-State sources. This choice is often seen as having significance.

If we turn first to non-State resources, one important source of funding in Ireland for organisations representing the poor – though probably less so for organisation *of* the poor - is benefactors or philanthropies such as Atlantic Philanthropy.

A second source of non-State resources is existing, well-resourced organisations that in some sense share the same concerns or values, or have some shared interest with the interest of people who are poor. In this way, the Trade Union movement was a significant source of support at various times for the unemployed organisations. Various Christian churches play an analogous role in providing resources for organisations addressing homelessness.

Clearly there are 'strings attached' to such support, whether explicit or implicit. A number of trade unions played a crucial role in the formation of the INOU in the late 1980s – the then Federated Workers Union of Ireland (FWUI) providing offices and funding; LGPSU providing funding for the wages of the first year, the electricians union, TEEU, providing offices from 1990 to 1994 and so on (Allen, 1996). From one perspective, this support can be seen to emerge from a political understanding: that there is a common interest between workers who are *in work* and those who are not. It derives from the historical tradition of solidarity within the Labour Movement. But there are more practical trade-offs. Trade union support for unemployed

71

organisations can be seen as an attempt to neutralise their impact on the day-to-day issues where the interests of those in work and those seeking work come into conflict – primarily the setting of wage levels.

A further example, which would reward deeper analysis from this perspective, is the development of Traveller organisations in Ireland. Early Traveller organisations were sponsored by elements within the Catholic Church that would have seen themselves as progressive, operating through the Parish of the Travelling People. These organisations conceived of progress for Travelling people to be assimilated into the settled community (Crowley and Kitchin 2007). From the 1980s, under the influence of ideas about ethnicity and identity, new organisations emerged, such as Pavee Point and later the Irish Traveller Movement. These new organisations argued that leadership should be provided by Travellers themselves and so represented a shift from 'organisations for the poor' into 'organisations of the poor.' They also argued for the separate ethnic identity of Travelling people and maintenance of a nomadic lifestyle. At least in their crucial early stages these new organisations obtained resources from the EU anti-poverty programmes and this provided the opportunity for them to break away from the traditional conceptual model of the earlier funders.

Ireland has, in the last few decades, provided a fairly broad range of opportunities for State funding for marginalised groups from employment schemes, community development funding and specific social partnership programmes. Employment schemes were key to the establishment of the INOU in the early 1980s. There is now a long experience of the implications of State funding for organisations of marginalised people. In the current crisis there is a widespread belief that such state funding is increasingly contingent on toning down of criticism of Government policy (Advocacy Initiative 2010).

Some of the commentary around this is, I believe, a little simplistic and assumes a simple trade-off between State resources and the abandonment of radical demands. From experience I know the relationship to be more complex. Within the INOU, for instance, I do not believe that there is a single point from 1987 to 2000, where we made a significant decision which would have been different if we had not been in receipt of State money.

This is not to say that dilemmas do not arise, it is rather to say that they are more likely to concern tensions between long-term relationships and goals and short-term impacts than they are to be about funding. Much more significant, I would argue, is the long-run effects of funding sources on where the organisation invests its energy. An organisation that is dependent upon its members for its resources is inevitably structured to engage and respond to their needs and expectations. Where resources are derived externally, there is greater independence from the day-to-day interests of the members and a greater focus on the needs of the funder.[18] Since organisations of the poor are always compelled to seek external resources this issue constantly emerges whatever the external source.

In their early days, organisations might be willing to risk loss of resources, but as the organisation matures and more people become dependent on it for services or employment, the nature potential constraining effect of funding shifts. Cathleen O'Neill of the Kilbarrack Community Project has spoken eloquently about becoming less willing to speak out because of a sense of responsibility for the job security of her Project's staff.

It is important to note that the lack of resources for organisations of poor people is not just about money; it is also about the capacities within the organising group itself. For instance, if we were establishing an organisation for unemployed people now we would be able to draw on a range of people with useful skills for say, establishing a web site. As things stand in the Irish labour market, we would have little trouble finding someone with experience and skills in this area.

However, in a number of years when the economy has recovered to some extent, or higher skilled people have emigrated, the situation will be different. People who have skills and ability are always more likely to escape unemployment than those who are without skills. So, over time, those who remain unemployed are less likely to be able to bring skills to the task of organising.

In communities where long-term unemployment has become endemic, people who are unemployed may not only lack necessary skills but may even not be in contact with anyone who does have them. In Ireland in the 1980 and 90s people might grow up not even knowing anyone who had a job.

---

[18] There are parallels here with the impact of State funding for political parties on the relationship with their grass roots which would be interesting to explore on another occasion.

A final element of this is the disempowerment that comes with long-term poverty, unemployment or homelessness. Morale and self-belief is a resource too. Long periods of not being able to find work, yet alone not having a place to live, leaves people with an overwhelming sense that they are powerless and their interventions are futile.

So, while RMT illuminates some central features of what makes social movements effective in modern liberal societies, it also draws attention to a process in which the very importance of civic society organisations in modern democracy can result in communities and individuals who are poor being left even further behind. By definition they are driven to seek external resources. While this does not inevitably silence their message, it involves them in a range of trade-offs and strategic choices, which have the potential to draw them away from their original intention.

New Movement Theory

A second major conceptual framework, which seeks to understand how social movements form and operate, is called New Movement Theory. The description is more than a little misleading as it is by no means a single theory, but a range of interacting and sometimes competing theories and it is by no means any longer 'new'.

While there are many strands of New Social Movements, they all contain this idea of some form of common identity being the central organising feature. Most of the significant and successful social movements in the developed world during the late 20th century follow this pattern: the women's movement, the gay and lesbian movement, the 'black power' strands within the civil rights movement, the disability rights movement.

New Social Movement Theory is rooted in European social theory traditions and emerges in response to two reductionist weaknesses in classical Marxism. The first weakness is the view that all politically significant social actions derive from the logic of capitalist production. The second is the view that the significant social actors are defined by their class relationships – other identities being secondary (Buechler 1995).

Understanding social movements in this way sheds some interesting light on the relationship between social movements of the unemployed and the Trade Union movement. If the most significant conflict in capitalism lies between labour and capital, the Trade Union movement must always seek to absorb movements of the unemployed and put them under their leadership. Unemployed movements are part of the 'labour side' of this conflict and unless their weight can be captured by Trade Unions, they will be used to undermine the bargaining power of the workers by driving down wages. You don't need to call yourself a Marxist to take this view, working within the Trade Union movement, or indeed employers' organisations would give this perspective in an un-intellectualised form. So the relationship with Trade Unions is crucial to unemployed organisations if the conflict over production is the central conflict in our society, but new social movements and their success show that other area of contestation – race, ethnicity, gender, sexual orientation – are of equal or greater importance and here victories can be won. This insight allows unemployed movements, frustrated with the failure of unions to provide solutions, to think of themselves in a different way and not simply place themselves as the agents of labour – or capital.

So these identity approaches to self-organisation, participation and power seem to offer exciting opportunities for organisations of the poor. For groups that tend to suffer poverty because of societal responses to their identity, particularly discrimination in the labour market, great progress can be made taking this approach. Much of the progress made by people with disabilities arises from this approach. Travellers might be another, though more problematic, example. Various forms of anti-discrimination legislation and practice can challenge these identity-based exclusions and increase access to employment and open up routes out of poverty.

However, when the group in question is defined by its very socio-economic condition – such as 'the unemployed' or 'the homeless' – a number of intractable difficulties arise.

These difficulties arise from the very nature of unemployment and homelessness. Both unemployment and homelessness are socio-economic conditions that are – or at least can and should be – transitory. In this respect, the poverty caused by old age or disability raises different types of demands than poverty caused by unemployment. A group representing the interests of the elderly poor will put forward demands aimed to stop being poor - not to stop being old. Radical, physical disability groups attempt to transform public attitudes to people with differing abilities and so change the social construction of disability, but they are not demanding to be themselves physically altered. This is not the case with unemployment and homelessness where the central demand is the right to escape from that condition.

This episodic or transitory nature of unemployment and homelessness has several consequences for attempts to build movements built on identity.

Most people who become unemployed think they will escape pretty quickly – and most of them are right. Most people who lose their jobs are re-employed fairly fast. The very poor data on homelessness in Ireland means that we cannot be certain that this is true of homelessness, but in the US we know from turn-over rates that most people who become homeless escape again in a short period (Culhane 2007).

This means not only that it is *difficult* to create a sense of common identity among people who are unemployed or homeless, in most cases it is pointless. They are gone before such an identity can be mobilised.

Even where people do not escape in that first period, the difficulties continue. Building a social movement on an identity of homelessness or unemployment is asking your members to construct their identity around something very damaging which is being done to them. Furthermore, it is something that they wish to stop happening and the desire to stop it happening is the very reason they want to form a social movement. It is hard to conceive of an invitation to this movement as anything other than an invitation to see yourself as a victim rather than a social actor.

A similar problem has been overcome in the networks of people who have experienced rape or abuse as children. Such support groups have tackled this effectively by insisting on the term 'survivor' rather than 'victim'. This shift in language asserts their commonality as a strength and implies that their personal identity is not subservient to their negative experience. However, even this does not provide a solution in the case of socio-economic exclusion. Survivor groups do not seek to create a common identity around something that is continuing to happen, but rather relate to an experience *in the past*, which has now been overcome.

Similar linguistic tactics have been used in other social movements to capture descriptions which were originally derogatory and degrading and turn them into a badge of identity. 'Gay Pride' is one example of this, while the use of the term 'cripple' or 'crip' by disability groups still remains challenging (Shakespeare 1993). But again this tactic is not transferable to the experience of people who are homeless or unemployed. These are both situations from which people wish to escape, not change social attitudes to. There are, of course, demands which will make it more bearable to be homeless or unemployed and representative groups put these forward, but ultimately people don't want to improve their experience of unemployment, they wish to escape the condition.

But the difficulties don't stop there. We know, in the case of homelessness, that 'self-identification' as homeless is actually a barrier to escaping homelessness (Christian 2003). I am not aware of any research on the labour market outcomes of 'self-identification as unemployed' but common sense would suggest it would catastrophically undermine any motivation in job seeking. This would indeed be the 'lifestyle choice' that the Minister for Social Protection, Joan Burton, has claimed to be prevalent among the long-term unemployed.

So even trying to form an organisation of people is not only difficult, it might well be deeply damaging to their future prospects.

All attempts to build user organisations on these shifting sands must find tactics to maintain organisational stability by retaining activists who have moved on from the experience (Anker 2008; Allen 2009; Williams 2005). However, this raises a series of difficult questions. The first is that it undermines one of the central claims of the organisation: that people who *are* *experiencing* unemployment/homelessness understand it best and shifts it to a claim that people who have, at some time, experienced unemployment/homelessness know best. This inevitably raises the question of what period of homelessness entitles you to how many years of 'representation'?

This approach also raises the question of whether those who wish to continue to speak on behalf of a condition they experienced in the past, or have continued to experience through choice, are in any way representative of all those others who have moved through and on? The implications of this question is that charismatic or opportunistic individuals may come to dominate the organisation, claiming a legitimacy based on an experience which is entirely atypical. To be recognised as the spokesperson for an excluded group may confer a social status that is not easily achieved by simply moving on into mainstream employment and putting the period of homelessness behind you. This challenge emerges in a number of case studies of homeless organisations (Williams 2005).

This is not just a theoretical question of the legitimacy of the individual who makes this choice, as I have written elsewhere in relation to the 'end of work' hypothesis, the different perspective of the person who chooses unemployment from the one who wishes to escape it, can have significant impact on public policy debates.

Poor People's Movements

The final conceptual framework I want to look at is the only one of which I am aware which actually attempts to specifically address the problems faced by the poor people's movement.

Piven and Cloward (1991), after reviewing a range of labour disputes, welfare and civil right campaigns in the USA, concluded that the only impact poor people can have is to disrupt the 'normal' operation of society.

They also recognised that the occasions in which movements of the poor arise are rare. They set out a number of explanations for this, some of which have much in common with the issues I have raised above with RMT. In recognising how infrequently poor people spontaneously form social movements, however, they don't take the conventional Left approach of lamenting this and thinking of ways in which the poor could be encouraged to be more rebellious. Instead they emphasised the need to maximise the impact of any mobilisation when it does occur. They note that professional organisers respond to such outbreaks of social movement action by attempting to create formal organisations so that the initiative can be prolonged and formalised. At the height of the disruption, they spend their time registering members and creating structures. Piven and Cloward argue that this is counterproductive and distracts energies from what such outbreaks can do best – win demands through their power to disrupt (1991).

There is much that is challenging in this. I think they make a compelling case that the attempt to capture such occasional outbreaks into formal structures is often misplaced and unproductive, but I am not convinced that they demonstrate that it is the efforts to create sustainable organisations which causes the dissipation of energies. I suspect that the energies might, in many cases, dissipate at the same rate no matter what the organisers do.

A more significant question, however, is how these insights translate from the USA to Ireland. I think two issues arise. From the mid-1990 until 2008, it was not plausible to argue in Ireland that the only power available to organisations representing the poor was 'disruption'. There were wide-open channels to the highest level of decision making through Social Partnership and endless opportunities to have issues aired and addressed. Of course, looking back now, we can see that these Social Partnership channels did not allow the fundamental issues of equality and sustainability to be addressed. Whether this is a feature of the system or the failure of the particular representatives is matter for debate, but it is incontestable that these issues were not properly addressed. However, it is also true that the sort of structural issues that address inequality are also the least likely to be formulated as demands at a grassroots level. Piven and Cloward are clear that the sort of demands that lead to the potential to take disruptive action are more likely to relate to symptoms of underlying structural injustice rather than the causes themselves. Exactly the same sort of issue, in fact, that was discussed in Social Partnership, and fairly well progressed there, in their own limited terms.

The second issue that arises from the Piven and Cloward analysis for Ireland is the rarity of occasions of mobilisation. Rarity does not begin to describe it. I can't think of any time before the boom period, during the boom period or in the subsequent recession when I have seen any evidence of significant potential mobilisation by people who are poor to protect their own interests. Two cuts in welfare payments hardly raised a murmur. The only noticeable social movement mobilisation involved the mobilisation of largely poor pensioners to defend the right of better off pensioners to hold on to free medical treatment.

One way in which the Piven and Cloward perspective can help us to understand the Irish situation is if we take a much broader view of what we mean by disruption. Their analysis revolves around civil disobedience and street protest, but there are other ways to disrupt the 'normal running' of society. I think there is a strong case to be made that the capacity of the INOU to force itself into Social Partnership and to make initial gains there derives directly from its capacity to 'disrupt' processes that were seen as crucial to economic success if they were excluded (Larragy 2004). Equally the loss of that power to 'disrupt' led to loss of potency within Social Partnership and a growing irrelevance.

The power that the unemployed had in the mid-1990s was a capacity to disrupt Social Partnership itself. This power arose because of the failure of the agreements up until that point to generate jobs or raise welfare levels. On the outside, the INOU could undermine the legitimacy of the agreement and specifically influence sufficient trade union members to reject any agreement. The traditional social partners and Government needed a new agreement and so had to invite in the unemployed to prevent this threatened disruption. Many other community sector organisations were drawn into social partnership at this time, but they never had either the capacity or willingness to cause such disruption. Even by the time of the partnership agreement in 2000, with an employment boom in full swing, this power had weakened; and certainly by 2003 when a number of Community and Voluntary Sector organisations refused to sign the partnership deal, dissent from this quarter was not even embarrassing, let alone disruptive: they were shown the door and business went on as normal.

Seeing the decade long engagement of the Community and Voluntary sector in Social Partnership within this 'disruptive' framework moves away from the lamentation that it was a strategic error for the 'sector' and begins to focus attention on what was and could have been achieved.

Conclusion

The question of how people who are poor can exercise network power through social movements is not a marginal issue. The barriers that the homeless and unemployed have faced in making their voice heard will confront a much larger proportion of humanity as winner-takes-all capitalism develops. Castells argues that 'the most fundamental divide in the network society, albeit not the only one, is between self-programmable labour and generic labour' (Castells 2009: 30). The terms require little further explanation. Self-programmable labour is educated, skilled and creative. Generic labour is assigned the 'tasks that are little valued, yet necessary … eventually replaced by machines or shifted to lower cost production sites.' Since generic labour comprises the 'overwhelming mass of working people on the planet' it clearly goes well beyond my concept of 'people who are poor.' But in a sense the position of people who are unemployed, and particularly those who are homeless, is an extreme case of Castells 'generic labour.' He predicts that 'They are disposable, unless they assert their rights to exist as humans and citizens through their collective action.' Yet they are the very people for whom collective action is the most difficult.

Some years ago the broadcaster and journalist Vincent Browne was asked who his heroes are in Irish society. Browne, who has a well known interest in social justice and equality, said that his three heroes are Stanislaus Kennedy, founder of Focus Ireland; Sean Healy, formerly of Conference of Religious in Ireland now founder of Social Justice Ireland; and Peter McVerry, campaigner for young and homeless working class people and founder of the Peter McVerry Trust.

After two decades in which the moral credibility of the Catholic Church has been systematically undermined by waves of revelations and by its own behaviour, the three Church figures who retain credibility are those who stand at the head of social movements for the poor.

I don't contest Browne's list. After almost three decades of building community organisations in disadvantaged communities, I contend there is not a single person from such a background who could plausibly be added to that list. Neither is there a single professional from a non-religious background. In twenty years time, when those figures are gone will there be any figures to replace them and if so where will they have emerged from?

This raises for me the question of whether we are looking in the right place or even looking for the right things. If the power of the unemployed in the early 1990s was in fact the power to threaten to disrupt, but what we could most usefully threaten was not the traffic on O'Connell Street but social partnership, what should we be seeking to disrupt now, and what should be our price for not doing so?

We are rightly concerned about participation and we have long experience of the way in which excluding marginalised people from discussions about their problems creates deeper problems. But I worry that when we make participation a moral imperative for people who are marginalised and poor, we are maybe just creating another barrier to prevent us addressing the injustice that their condition represents. I think most people who consider themselves 'progressive' are deeply critical of the view that the unemployed just need to 'get on their bikes' or that it is up to the homeless man to pull himself together. We understand that those forms of exclusion are structural and systematic and require societal change if they are to be addressed. Yet we still seem to retain the notion that such societal change requires that marginalised groups self-organise and participate in their own struggle. We trap ourselves in a form of Social Movement Social Darwinism.

I have discussed social movements of poor people in the context of political social movements that have successfully raised both a political question and provided its answer. They 'agenda set' and 'problem solve'; they demand that society recognises that the condition of, say, black people is unacceptable and propose that legislative or social change occur to address this. It is possible that insurmountable problems that arise in poor peoples organisations emerge when they aim to take on both those tasks. This concern leaves us with the possibility that, if we hope to see the elimination of poverty, unemployment and homelessness, it will actually fall to people who are not poor, homeless or unemployed to do something about it. It has to be a broader coalition of forces within society that must declare these things unacceptable. Individuals and movements of excluded people can then emerge to bring forward some of the right answers. But an approach to the politics of participation that even half believes that it is up to the poor to get the question raised is condemning us to a perpetually unequal society.

CHAPTER 8
ADVANCING BIOMEDICAL RESEARCH: EXPLORING INTERACTIONS BETWEEN SCIENTISTS, SCIENCE COMMUNICATORS AND THE PUBLIC

Emma O'Brien

Introduction

This paper explores Ireland's scientific and technology transformation, with a focused look on the significant investment made by Irish Government's since the late 1990s in Science, Technology and Innovation. It looks at the development of new State agencies such as Science Foundation Ireland, the National Foundation for Investment in Scientific and Technological Research. Drawing on the literature, this paper highlights the historical lack of Irish public engagement with science policy. However, it notes there has been a significant increase and public participation in science engagement initiatives in the past decade. This paper explores a number of such programs. It presents a case study of one biomedical science research institute, the Biomedical Diagnostics Institute, which through its education and outreach programme promotes the concept of Scientific Citizenship, providing citizens with the competencies, knowledge and skills to interact with science and technologies that extensively shape everyday life.

Science Policy in Ireland

In 1996, the Irish Government produced the first ever extended statement of formal science policy in the history of the state. After the development of this white paper, a new policy advisory body, The Irish Council for Science, Technology and Innovation (ICSTI), was established and was set the goal to produce Ireland's first Technology Foresight Report (Trench 2003).

Ireland's first technology foresight exercise was an intensive study whereby dozens of leaders in Government, academic and industry assessed the Irish economy, from pharmaceuticals to life science, from transportation to manufacturing. They asked how might these areas evolve over the long term? The assessment concluded that biotechnology and information communications technology represented "the engines of future growth in the global economy"

(ICSTI 1999: 7). The report led directly to the allocation of significant funding to carry out research in biotechnology and information communications technology. In 2000, Science Foundation Ireland (SFI) was established to oversee the delivery of these funds.

Simultaneously, a number of other state agencies, such as the Higher Education Authority (HEA), were initiating a fundamental change in how academic research was funded, with the aim of transforming the country's global reputation and output in science and engineering.

The Programme for Research in Third Level Institutions (PRTLI) was established by the HEA in 1998 and was central to the rapid development of research and development in Irish universities and other institutes of higher education. To date the programme has awarded €1.22 billion (including exchequer and private matching funds) in strengthening national research capabilities via investment in human and physical infrastructure. The programme supports research in humanities, science, technology and the social sciences including business and law.

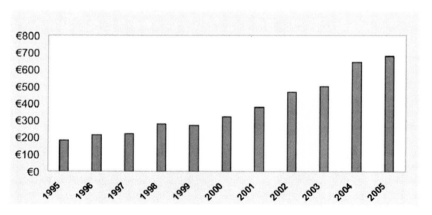

Figure 3: Government expenditure on STI 1995-2005 in public and private sectors (constant prices).
Source: Strategy for Science, Technology and Innovation 2006-2103 (Government of Ireland 2006).

In the preceding years, the Irish Government made a major commitment, through substantial public investment in science, technology and innovation which resulted in Ireland making great strides in growing capabilities in this field.

In 2006, Ireland's Strategy for Science, Technology and Innovation (2006-2013) was launched. The guiding principle of the Strategy for Science, Technology and Innovation (SSTI) was that excellence in research and increased innovation in the enterprise sector could help accelerate Ireland's economic restructuring and help on the path of sustainable growth. The Government made a major commitment, through substantial public investment, in the SSTI with the result that significant steps were made in establishing a strong research environment, based on building scientific excellence in a number of key strategic areas. The stated aim at the launch of the strategy was that:

Ireland by 2013 will be internationally renowned for the excellence of its research, be at the forefront in generating and using new knowledge for economic and social progress, within an innovation driven culture (SSTI 2006: 8).

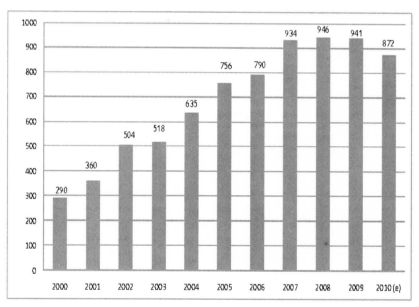

Figure 4: Government Sector Expenditure on R & D (GBOARD- Government Budget Appropriations or Outlays on R & D) 2000-2010.
Source: Research and Development Funding in the State Sector 2009-10 (Forfás 2011a).

The Government reinforced the importance of the investment in the SSTI in *Building Ireland's Smart Economy – A Framework for Sustainable Economic Renewal* (December 2008), which prioritised continued investment in science and engineering infrastructure and research. In 2009, the Government announced the appointment of an Innovation Taskforce to advise the Government on its Strategy for positioning Ireland as an International Innovation Hub and to assist in making the Smart Economy a reality. Whilst there was recognition of economic difficulties, the Report from the Innovation Taskforce in March 2010, noted that level of investment in STI should not be diminished and further investment in an SSTI for 2014-2020 should be committed to (Innovation Taskforce 2010).

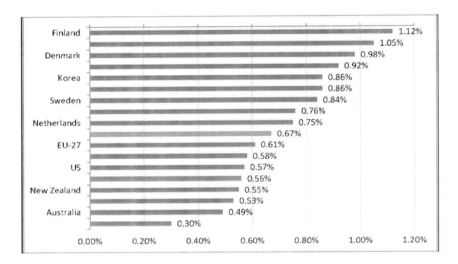

Figure 5: International comparison of Government expenditure on R&D as a percentage of GDP/GNP (2010). Irish Government expenditure (highlighted in green) at 0.67 per cent of GNP is greater than the EU 27 countries average of 0.61 per cent.
Source: Science, Technology and Innovation Indicators (Forfás 2011b).

Measuring the return on investment

In the publication of the Science, Technology and Innovation Indicators (Forfás 2011b), it was noted that in the last decade Ireland trebled the level of investment in research and development, providing enterprise support for R&D, investing in human capital, physical infrastructure and the commercialisation of research. The investment made in the past decade, building upon complementarity between SFI, PRTLI, Enterprise Ireland (EI), The Health Research Board (HRB), and other research funders, has brought about a steep change in the research environment in Ireland. The overarching aim is to generate knowledge that will bring economic benefits and societal value to Ireland.

This investment has contributed significantly to an increase in Foreign Direct Investment, the increased competitiveness of indigenous enterprise and to the creation and application of new knowledge and technologies (SSTI Indicators, 2011). As the investment has continued, it is now possible to obtain key indicators for monitoring progress on the investment in Science, Technology and Innovation. Ireland currently ranks in the top 20 nations for quality of scientific publications. Ireland's citation impact is now 25% higher than the world average, Ireland is ranked 8th among 20 leading countries and is recognized as a leader in a number of areas including agriculture, immunology and material science (nanotechnology). Other indicators include an increase in patent output, in many cases marking the movement of discoveries toward the market or clinic, an increase in industry collaborations between researchers and industry and the development of new and innovative Irish companies.

The next section will look at the core theme of participation through one of the science funding agencies, Science Foundation Ireland (SFI) and, in particular, will look at its main programme of funding for the Centres for Science, Engineering & Technology (CSET) Programme.

Science Foundation Ireland

SFI was established in 2000 and is the state agency founded to manage investment of public funds into fundamental and applied research in the life sciences, information communication and emergent technologies and sustainable energy and energy efficient technologies. The agency resides within the Department of Jobs, Enterprise & Innovation (DJEI).

Despite the current economic circumstances, the Irish Government has continued strong investment in SFI with a funding investment of €161m in 2011 and just a 3% decrease in funding for 2012 to €156m.

SFI's biggest research investment is in Centres for Science, Engineering & Technology (CSETs). This funding programme began in 2003, with a funding commitment of €245m. The overarching aim of the CSET programme is to encourage research that brings together academic and industrial partners. The public investment involves a cost sharing with industry which is normally represented through an investment in people.

CSETS help link scientists and engineers in partnership across academia and industry to address crucial research questions, foster the development of new and existing Irish–based technology companies, attract industry that could make an important contribution to Ireland and its economy and expand education and career opportunities in science and engineering. In addition, each CSET centre has a significant education and public outreach remit.[19]

The Hub of Innovation

Etzkowitz (2008) proposes the innovation model of the Triple Helix. He defines how this hub of university-industry-government interaction is the key to innovation in increasingly knowledge-based societies. In this model, the government is the source of funding and acts as the source of contractual relations that guarantee stable interactions and exchange, the university is the arena for the generation of new knowledge and technologies whilst industry remains a key actor as the locus of production and commercialisation. Each can "take the role of the other" in triple helix interactions, however, there is great strength in their interactions from an innovation and knowledge generation perspective (Etzkowitz 2008: 74).

Such interactions are at the core of the SFI CSET model and have made significant contributions to Ireland from a societal and economic perspective. The next section will take a look at one of these CSET centres – The Biomedical Diagnostics institute (BDI), Dublin City University and explore how the institute is advancing biomedical research through interactions with scientists, science communicators and the general public.

---

[19] There are currently nine funded CSETS in Ireland:
- The Alimentary Pharmabiotic Centre at University College Cork;
- The Digitial Enterprise Research Institute at National University of Ireland, Galway;
- The Centre for Research on Adaptive Nanostructures & Nanodevices, Trinity College Dublin;
- The Centre for Telecommunications Value-Chain-Driven Research, Trinity College Dublin;
- Lero-Irish Software Engineering Research Centre, University of Limerick;
- The Biomedical Diagnostics Institute, Dublin City University;
- The Centre for Next Generation Localisation, Dublin City University;
- Clarity Research Centre, University College Dublin;
- Systems Biology Ireland, University College Dublin.

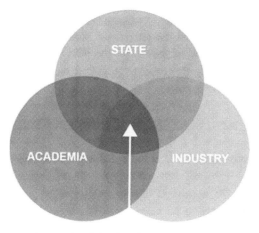

Innovation Stimulated at the Focal Point

Figure 6: Triple Helix model of Innovation (Etzkowitz, 2008).

The Biomedical Diagnostics Institute

The Biomedical Diagnostics Institute (BDI) is a SFI CSET centre. Established in October 2005, the BDI is an Academic-Industrial-Clinical partnership that carries out research focused on the development of next-generation biomedical diagnostic devices. The Institute is hosted at Dublin City University.

The Institute was established to transform healthcare through translation of research in diagnostic science and technology into clinical utility. Early diagnosis and on-going monitoring of patients undergoing therapy is central to the successful treatment of major diseases, especially cancer, cardiovascular disease and acute infection. The BDI is addressing these issues head-on by developing highly sensitive methods of detecting markers of disease in small sample volumes, typically a patient's blood, at high speed and critically, at low cost. Through its clinical and industrial partners, these solutions are optimised for efficient transfer to the patient.

To achieve these goals, BDI has formed an internationally distinctive partnership between world-leading academic, clinical and industrial teams (the partnership includes five universities, three hospitals and four industrial partners). Uniquely, this structure allows scientific research to be directly informed by clinicians who treat patients and have a deep understanding of their needs. The discoveries generated, for example detection of cancer cells in the blood of a patient, can be rapidly translated to the clinic and then commercialised through BDI's industrial partners. In this way, the BDI is able to bring its efforts in diagnostic research to the market and to have a direct effect on how disease is detected and treated.

<u>Education & Outreach (E & O) at the Biomedical Diagnostics Institute</u>
The BDI has developed a comprehensive and innovative biomedical education programme, which is far reaching and enables BDI educators and scientists to interact with students of all ages and the general public. Over 23,000 students have participated across the various initiatives, exposing them to the scientific discovery in the biomedical science and health field. The BDI's education & outreach laboratory provides a learning space and central focus for education and outreach activities within the Institute.

The education and outreach programme has been developed based upon relationships formed between BDI educators, scientists and science communicators. The programme content is guided by insights from students, teachers, the local community and education specialists. Novel initiatives have been developed based upon collaboration with industry, entrepreneurs, learning innovators and digital researchers.

There is a key focus on programme evaluation, which has been tailored toward each activity and provides meaningful insight. Programme evaluation enables the E & O team to monitor and amend initiatives and to gauge impacts. A mixed-methods approach is applied to all evaluation.

Highlights of the BDI's public engagement programme will be described in the next section. However, first it is important to explore the motivations for encouraging public engagement in both science and technology and science policy in Ireland.

Public engagement and interest in Science & Science Policy

As noted earlier, since the late 1990s the Government has firmly committed Ireland on a pathway toward a knowledge economy. This has been the underlying policy objectives of many initiatives in the broader economic sphere and in the specific domains of education, research and innovation. However, as noted by (Trench 2003) and the *Monitoring Policy and Research Activities on Science in Europe* (MASIS) *National Report - Ireland* (2011) this policy commitment to the knowledge economy and the related increase in public investment have not been much debated in the political sphere and have been achieved with minimum public participation.

Up to 2008, there were few public commentaries on the knowledge economy that were not a positive endorsement of the strategy. However, the returns on investment as outlined in section 1 have become a topic of more active debate since the economic recession erupted in 2008. Expenditure across all Government Departments and public agencies are at the centre of public and political debates. By extension, the Governments' investment in scientific research has come under scrutiny (MASIS 2011).

Furthermore, recent Eurobarometer studies (European Commission 2010c) indicate although the majority of Irish people surveyed believe science can improve their lives, they have a lower level of interest in scientific issues and feel less well informed when compared with other EU states.

Science Citizenship

From a review of the literature (Davies and Wolf-Philips 2006), it is evident that recent years have witnessed a 'democratic turn' toward active participation in science and technology (Mejlgaard and Stares 2010). The idea of Scientific Citizenship has been promoted as a useful method to bridge the divide between concerns about public participation and public competence and engagement with science, technology and related policy. Horst (2007: 151) provides the following definition of Scientific Citizenship:

> The notion of Scientific Citizenship (Irwin 2001) points to an increasing awareness of the intermingling between science and society. It implies not only that scientific knowledge is important for citizenship in contemporary society but also that citizens can lay a legitimate claim about accountability on scientific research. As such, the notion can be perceived as a normative ideal concerning the appropriate form of democratic governance in a society that has become increasingly dependent on scientific knowledge.

Mejlgaard and Stares (2010) note that in many of our modern economics, science and technologies extensively shape the everyday lives of the public and affect social practices and citizens are in need of particular competencies, knowledge and skills to navigate effectively and define their role within the system. Furthermore, Kolsto (2001) notes that in democratic societies, the quality of the decisions made by the laity is of fundamental importance. Lay people's ability to promote their point of view on socio-scientific issues are therefore significant (Kolsto 2001). Scientific Citizenship thus enables citizen competence in the sciences, but also encourages active participation in debate.

Citizen involvement in Science and Science Policy in Ireland

There are no formal procedures for individual citizens or civil society organisations (CSOs) to take part in priority setting and assessment activities with regard to science and technology in Ireland. Citizen volunteerism and CSO participation are strong in many areas of cultural, social and sporting life, but not as strong in political life, outside of political parties. Science and Technology matters are rarely on the agenda of the houses of parliament, neither of which have a committee dedicated to monitoring and discussing Science and technology issues (MASIS 2011).

There are, however, a significant number of science in society and public engagement initiatives underway in Ireland through Government funded agencies such as Discover Science & Engineering (DSE), the education and outreach programmes of the CSET centres funded by SFI and through a number of other university and higher education institutions such as CALMAST at Waterford Institute of Technology and the Science Gallery at Trinity College Dublin.

The MASIS report (2011) notes that there has been a significant increase in participation in public science initiatives in the past decade, albeit mainly concentrated in well-educated, urban, younger sectors of the population

It is also worthy of note, that in the latest OECD PISA (Programme for International Student Assessment) Study, 2009, an international assessment of the knowledge and skills of 15-year-olds in reading, mathematics and science, Ireland ranked 14th highest of 34 OECD countries and 20th highest of the 65 participating countries in overall science performance. Overall, Ireland's mean score is still significantly above the OECD average (Perkins *et al.* 2010).

Whilst significant research has been carried out on science policy informing "dialogue events", science dialogue events that do not seek to inform public policy are under researched, even though as highlighted above these are increasing in growth and popularity in

Ireland and Europe. Davies et al (2009) argue that it is valuable to frame and evaluate dialogue events in terms of symmetrical social learning. Thus, dialogue events that do not seek to influence policy are spaces enabling individuals from potentially diverse cultures to come together, articulate positions and views, and interact in a context of genuine equality. It could even be argued that this could, theoretically, be a far more effective way of affecting the culture of science to become more personally relevant and democratically accountable than through public participation in policy (Davis et al, 2009).

The next sections highlights a number of projects underway at the BDI, which highlight good practice in terms of public engagement in science and promoting active science citizenship.

Examples of Good Practice

The Debating Science Issues (DSI) project which aims to enable policy engagement in an informal manner is an interactive, science dialogue programme where young people are invited to engage in debate and discussion on the cultural, societal and ethical implications of advances in biomedical science. The first of its kind in Ireland, DSI is an all-Ireland debating schools competition aimed at senior cycle students with a number of secondary audiences (including post-primary teachers, parents and families, science researchers and the general public). The programme led by the Regenerative Medicine Institute at NUIG, has run for five years and is funded through a Public Engagement Award from the Wellcome Trust. It involves partnership with collaborators involved in biomedical research and education expertise across Ireland.[20]

Since inception over 200 post-primary schools have taken part in the Debating Science Issue programme, and over 3,000 students have

---

[20] These include:

- Regenerative Medicine Institute, National University of Ireland, Galway;
- Biomedical Diagnostics Institute, Dublin City University;
- Alimentary Pharmabiotic Centre, University College Cork;
- The Centre for Research on Adaptive Nanostructures & Nanodevices, Trinity College Dublin;
- Clarity Research Centre, University College Dublin;
- Cork Institute of Technology;
- W5 Belfast;
- Royal College of Surgeons in Ireland, Dublin;
- Centre for Cross Border Studies, Armagh.

participated in the Debating competition. Student participation in DSI begins with a three hour bioethical workshop delivered in schools by the project partners. Students engage in discussion in an impartial, round table forum exploring stakeholders views and the surrounding issues. The workshop is based upon the Democs discussion format (a conversation game that helps small groups to discuss public policy issues). The DSI partnership have developed Democs kits for each of the scientific topics discussed including Health & Self Testing, Nanotechnology, Immunology, Rare Disease, Stem Cell research. The Democs format helps participants understand the issues associated with a topic before giving their opinions. Harnessing the enthusiasm gained, a schools' dynamic debate competition ensues throughout all four provinces of Ireland. Debaters are challenged to defend their positions before judges, teachers, and peers.

As part of the programme both formative and summative evaluation is carried out. In 2011, the workshops involved 637 students and 438 progressed to the debating arm of the competition. 88 debate judges were involved. 89% of participating students agreed that from discussing the research topics, they understood how scientific knowledge and ideas can change over time. Following the workshops, 76% of students felt that "after discussing the topic, I feel I can better evaluate the impact of scientific developments or processes on people, communities or the environment. 86% of participants felt that the topics explored made them think about scientific or technical developments, and their benefits, drawbacks and risks. Interestingly, 75% of students surveyed at debate rounds, reported discussing the science and issues outside of school with family and friends.

88 debate judges were involved, some of whom judged more than one round of debates. One judge in the 2011 Leinster debate commented:

I think one of the things that most impressed me was the ability of the students to deal with some very complex and emotive issues, some of which older and more experienced professionals would have found difficult to debate! It was great that they were willing to take this on. I also found it very inspiring to know that there are many younger people who are willing to take part and who are interested in science.

The partners are striving to further enhance the project through inclusion in curriculum and other public events. In 2012, the DSI project website was enhanced through the incorporation of social media for further public engagement including, the project's own TV channel, live feeds and link to Twitter and Facebook.

Democs has been adapted into *PlayDecide - Your Future Health - Is it a good idea to know your risks?* This web-based project makes discussion kits on science topics available for download across Europe. The project is being led by FUND, which is a two-year project supported by the European Commission to stimulate the use of discussion games and other debate formats in European cities for the development of a scientific culture at the local level. The goal of FUND is to facilitate the take-up of participatory methods, exchange experiences and knowledge, and embed them in the ongoing activities of actors who interface the public with the governance of science: local administrations, museums, universities, networks, associations, community groups, NGOs, public/private research organizations etc.

In Winter 2010, the BDI's Education team, received funding through the FUND project to develop a Play Decide kit that would facilitate discussion around Health & Diagnostic Testing in the local community. The kit focused around health risk, which if can be identified early can prevent the onset of a serious medical event. Identifying risk early for medical conditions such as cardiovascular disease and diabetes is beneficial for both the patient and the health service. However, there is a lot involved in understanding health risks, there is much in the covered in the media on the topic of risk factors and steps that can be taken to reduce risk, but is this information helpful or does it lead to confusion? The BDI education team sought to adapt and replace the original text-rich format with multimedia elements appropriate for adults with low reading and writing competence and non-native English speakers. The aim of the project was to promote debate and discussion on diabetes, cardiovascular disease and disease risk factors. Following collaboration with BDI ethics researchers in the development of supplementary content, the multimedia elements compiled included a video clip of an advertisement for a cholesterol-reducing spread, a radio clip on health screening and an over-the-counter home cholesterol test kit. Three events were run with adult groups in the local community. A detailed evaluation was carried out to observe if the new multimedia content sparked discussions. This evaluation helped in the adaptation of a number of the elements in the kit for future use and highlighted the effectiveness of some in particular, including the over-the-counter kit for cholesterol testing. It was evident that the topic of heart health and the positive effects of a healthy lifestyle to reduce risk were important and relevant to those that participated. Many relevant concerns were voiced, such as what is a healthy lifestyle, and much factual information was shared, for example on the meaning of cholesterol levels.

These events showed that the *PlayDecide* game is a useful tool to engage groups of adults with topics of personal and societal importance such as health and health research. During the events, participants had the opportunity to discuss the issue of cardiovascular disease in a relaxed and non-judgmental environment. A large amount of general factual information on heart disease, healthy living and risk factors was communicated to the group, predominantly stemming from questions from group members. This shows that the game can help to tailor health information to a particular group, based on their own concerns and knowledge gaps. The education team intend to utilize the play decide format in upcoming public engagement activities.

The BDI has established a Diagnostics and Society research programme, which has been developed in collaboration with School of Nursing, Dublin City University. This research aims to integrate ethical and social scientific research methodologies with BDI research programmes. There are currently two projects underway, the first project focuses around cardiovascular disease and the potential for patient use of a risk chip which would indicate propensity toward the disease. The second project looks at self-testing devices and their implications for patient autonomy in healthcare. Both of these projects are currently in trials with patients and the public and further research is underway. The findings of these research projects will directly feed into BDI research programs and impact on end user technology development. These projects demonstrate ambitious efforts to bring ethical and societal issues into scientific research.

The Future

Ireland has seen unprecedented growth in investment in Science, Technology and Innovation in the past decade, with an overarching aim to generate knowledge that will bring economic benefit and societal value to Ireland. It is now possible to obtain key indicators to monitor the success of this investment. There is evidence that the quantity and quality of publicly performed research has increased significantly as judged by most of the key Science, Technology and Innovation indicators (e.g. R&D intensity, publication rates, citation rates, human capital, etc.). In most cases, we have moved from a below world average position to being at or above the relevant world averages.

At the time of writing, the government is set to shortly publish the results of a 2011 research prioritisation exercise, which will identify priority areas for the next phase of Ireland's Science, Technology and Innovation strategy. This paper has noted the historical lack of public engagement with science policy and Irish people's lower level of interest in scientific issues in comparison to other EU countries. However, there is significant scope to enhance future STI strategy by increasing public participation in science through public engagement initiatives.

In 2012, Dublin was designated European City of Science and hosted the Euroscience Open Forum. An ambitious public science engagement program provided scope for public engagement with science in a city context throughout the year. While there is currently committed public funding for Science, Technology and Innovation to 2014, the current economic situation has made future sustained commitment at a high level unpredictable. The new EU framework programme for research and innovation, Horizon 2020, will run from 2014 to 2020 with an €80 billion budget. Horizon 2020, provides Ireland with an excellent opportunity to sustain and grow scientific endeavour of benefit to society whilst also promising to deepen the relationship between science and society. Horizon 2020 will favour an informed engagement of citizens and civil society on research and innovation matters by promoting science education, by making scientific knowledge more accessible, by developing responsible research and innovation agendas that meet citizens' and civil society's concerns and expectations and by facilitating their participation in Horizon 2020 activities.

CHAPTER 9
DIALOGIC SCIENCE AND DEMOCRACY: THE CASE OF NANOTECHNOLOGY

Padraig Murphy

Introduction

Nanotechnology, we are told, is an area of great promise for society (Forfás 2010; European Commission 2005). At this time of crisis in Ireland and Europe, however, all promissory tales told by governments and institutions need to be placed under scrutiny. In this chapter, I look at an emerging system of interdisciplinary research and development in Ireland that has evolved under the 'smart economy' and 'innovation' banners, an area of connected technological approaches collectively called 'nanotechnology'. Nanotechnology has wide political support globally (Hullman 2006), and in these challenging times, is increasingly linked in developed economies to national recovery and global technology strategies (Forfás 2012). It has been called an emerging, disruptive technology (*ibid.*) However, while opposition is not evident in Ireland (Murphy 2010), NGOs and policymakers internationally urge caution against what some see as hype or misplaced promise at best, and potential health, environmental and ethical implications at worst (Friends of the Earth 2010). While the inclusion of NGOs in discussions about any technology is increasingly seen as a more dialogic way of developing technology (Felt *et al.* 2007) – particularly with local and international protests over emerging technologies such as genetically modified foods, energy technologies, and many others- civic society organisations are not necessarily the gatekeepers of public opinion. It is for this reason that this chapter argues for broadening inclusivity to include diverse publics, including the marginalised voices in society, to explore the true democratic potential of a potentially pervasive emerging technology and its associated nanoscience research.

How do we mean 'democratic' and 'dialogic' when referring to something supposedly universal such as science? This chapter will look at nanotechnology in an Irish context drawing from current thinking in science communication and science studies, particularly ideas concerning public engagement and public participation in science governance. The specific approach used here extends the concept of engagement to include how publics might interact and potentially shape the discourses, and indeed even the 'products', of emerging science. I will address two key areas: first, a separation between a strategic science and a constructed 'public' where public participation might happen, on the one hand operating as a one-way communication process but now increasingly dialogic, yet on the other hand also increasingly the context for strategic vision for Ireland in a global economy. We are in the era of *technoscience,* application-driven science with extraordinary epistemological position of legitimacy and public resonance (Nowotny *et al.* 2001). 'The public' here is often constructed as 'disadvantaged' in the sense of having a knowledge deficit, requiring education and more scientific literacy. Second, I ask why and where public participation should occur for something as abstract and technical as the nanosciences among communities that are truly disadvantaged in a social and economical sense, removed as they are from hi-tech policy discourses. However, there has, in recent decades, been greater emphasises in science communication theory and practice on public engagement (Wynne 2005; Dalgado 2010). I will focus on the citizen jury as one potentially strong, public -oriented model, drawing from an Environmental Protection Agency project on which I worked (Murphy, 2010). The chapter concludes with a description of how a sub-political dialogue, contributing to social action beneath mainstream politics, can best be achieved in an Irish context and how policy could realistically change in response to public response to nanotechnology.

Nanotechnology is a curious area, fractured into several areas of discourse. It became a talking point globally in the mid-2000s. Yet the talking was arguably of an elite nature. A UK report by the Royal Society and the Royal Academy of Engineering (2004) was the first major scientific policy document in this part of the world that recommended social, ethical and environmental considerations when pursuing nanoscale research and development. There is a broad definition often presented. The terms 'nanoscience' and 'nanotechnology' describe a range of converging technological processes expected to impact greatly on our future lives. The terms are commonly grouped singularly as nanotechnology. In this field, the standard definition goes, atoms and molecules are manipulated at scales below 100 nanometres, about 1/50,000th the width of a human hair. Because of the difference in properties of all matter at this scale -

'the 'nanoscale' - technologists theorise that matter can be exploited, creating new types of processes and objects. Structures can be created in the lab that are unimaginably small, and durable.

Discourse around this can be quite futuristic, but there are current applications such as nanosensors used as medical devices in the body and nanomaterials for the electronics or microchip market and in textiles, cosmetics and sporting equipment, where materials called nanoparticles are often used. Nanowires and carbon nanotubes are future applications expected in the construction of materials with vastly superior strength and electrical properties than currently exist in nature. But such social disruption, however positive, also brings risk. There are also many policy initiatives globally which suggest something else about nanotechnology besides promise. For example, the National Science Foundation in the US has invested 5% of its 2012 budget to what is termed 'ELSI', ethical, legal and social issues (National Science Foundation 2012). The OECD has published guidelines for member countries on how to engage publics about nanotechnology (OECD Directorate for Science, Technology and Industry Committee for Science and Technological Policy 2008). There is, without question, a ground-breaking aspect to this technology. If this technology is likely to be all-pervasive, then it needs to be the subject of public discussion.

Technoscience Strategy and Public Engagement

Epistemologies, Ontologies and Institutions of Science

Science, in a traditional understanding of it, strives to be global, objective, consistent and non-contextual. It is presented as the ultimate objectivity, removed from public intervention. Increasingly, in the West, it provides ontological security; in Ireland, science has emerged from Catholic dogma, perhaps leaving less room for other worldviews. In short, we believe, as a society, in science and its applications in society. The theme of the Martin McEvoy seminar series to which this chapter contributes is the current democratic deficit that appears to be a central criticism of the European crisis. And the European Research Area wants more science, more innovation, more translation from knowledge processes in higher education into product and jobs. Against this backdrop, science is surely a common good? Of course, we do need more science and in this year, Dublin being the *ESOF* City of

Science, we celebrate Irish science and our world-class research (Forfás 2012).

However, all should now be put before public consideration, across Europe. Dialogue has been one of the key objectives for Dublin City of Science. Dialogue requires greater discussion between institutions of science and the rest of society. The time of accepting universally the unlimited progress of science is gone. The condition of late modernity in the 21st century presents challenges to the linear progression of science, a dominant model, one version of the history of science. The evidence for why this is not the case anymore lies in the myriad of epidemics, genomics, climate change, HIV, diffusion of politics and knowledge, mixed together. Also, in the knotted history of technological development (Bucchi 2004), there have been innovations that have been morally and socially destructive (science–based eugenics, the Manhattan project, environmental degradation since the Industrial Revolution) as well progressive (healthcare generally in the 20th century, environmental cleaning technologies, space and geological exploration).[21] This is not to say that nanotechnology is another Manhattan project. But there have been concerns internationally (RS/RAE 2005), rarely discussed in Ireland (Murphy 2010). 'Science' becomes ring-fenced from other discourses, particularly discourses of risk, as we shall see, and a discourse of scientific literacy prevails. In this sense, science then is a hegemony. But the counter-argument against concerns about hegemonic control are the very real, rationalist fears about the rise of so-called pseudoscience (e.g. any science-sounding descriptions of alternative medicines or nutrition), or responses like faith-based resistance to stem cells or evolution and concerns over climate denialism.

But for nanotechnology, faith and fiction are ambiguously tied to the science as scientists and science communicators struggle to separate the 'fact' from the 'fiction'. Nanotechnology has been described as being somewhat alien, making it difficult for a non-expert to visualise as well as define (Hayles 2004). This visual, epistemological issue with nanotechnology is a challenge for the real world. Science sociologist Steve Fuller notes how, in contrast to data coming from physics, the 'convergences sciences' (bio-, cogno-, info- and nanotechnologies) are

---

[21] The Manhattan Project was a research and development program, led by the United States with participation from the United Kingdom and Canada, that produced the first atomic bomb during World War II.

organised around an epistemology of predictable, reconstructable matter with an aim to lead to human enhancement and other ethical minefields (Fuller, 2011). But at least by portraying the nanoscale in terms of real objects we can - goes the theory - understand it better. In classroom discussions with senior level students, described briefly below as part of my EPA-funded public engagement project, when discussing nanodevices used for medical procedures within the body, the first thing that students tended to ask was: 'How can we get it out again?' (Murphy 2010).

From this point, the element of risk is introduced. But more tellingly, the question was never fully resolved – does it mean nanobots? Is it invisible? What actually *is* nanotechnology, they may persistently ask, even at the end of a detailed class on the subject. The standard process descriptions are therefore rendered meaningless, when it is expected to be part of so many future products in healthcare, electronics, cars, sportsgear, clothes, even our food packaging, as nanotechnologists tell us will occur. This is part of the challenge for scientists and media when communicating nanotechnology (Murphy 2009). When we narrowly define what nanotechnology is, there is a danger of reducing other meanings, including the idea of risk (Murphy 2010). And there are risks associated with nanotechnology, both health and environmental – the extent of which nanotoxicology studies continue to determine (Anderson *et al.* 2009; Donaldson *et al.* 2004), but also the three Es of the ethical, and what might be called issues of equity and the existential. In the early 2000s, social scientists and natural scientists associated with the National Nanotechnology Institute in the US identified a need to engage with a sceptical public, mindful also of resistance to GMO foods, which have threatened whole industries (Roco 2003; Roco and Bainbridge 2001). And while the young people in our classroom discussions were unaware of, and felt far away from, the discourses that have emerged about nanotechnology, the less-than-real pictures of future nanotechnology, painted by Roco *et al*, have used utopian and dystopian colours. Consider space elevators and 'grey goo' scenarios of Ray Kurzweil (2012), or engines of creation of futurist Eric Drexler (1986), tiny replicator robots taking over the world. Neither seem likely to our current common sense.

This makes nanotechnology an interesting test case for all other emerging technologies in this late modern environment, where institutions, according to Ulrich Beck (1994) and Anthony Giddens

(1994), have more 'reflexivity', introducing various perspectives on risk. 'Institutional reflexivity' is the phrase used by social theorists such as Beck and Giddens to describe the response by institutions, such as science centres, but also other mega-institutions of science itself, to the identification, construction and control of risks in late modernity. Lash describes this best as *self-confrontation* of institutions (Lash 1994). Contemporary risk theorists such as Wynne (2005) and Sandman (Sandman and Lanard 2005) also point out that the subjective and affective are integrated into opinion-forming and decision-making in the rationalist discourse of scientific, technical risk assessment. This point, in many ways, is controversial; are we to treat each perspective on nanotechnology as valid? This attention to competing perspectives in a place where science establishes *fact* may be what postmodernist agendas have helped shape within science studies; however it is not that diffuse or relativist – we need to ensure varying viewpoints are heading towards workable (if not always consensus-based) solutions, and processes, even products, or perhaps challenging common and long-held assumptions. These ways of visualising science as part of a wider culture is the domain of science studies. Just as we, as a society, often have a corpuscular view of the world, engaging with the 'nanoscale' as cultural theorists Katherine Hayles (2004) and Colin Milburn (2004) would say, is more than an epistemology, but also is an ontology of reduction.

However, in the European Research Area, a conglomerate of policy bodies, higher education institutions, industry and research centres, a new theme within European science policy is the idea of 'responsible innovation'. Responsible innovation demands ethics and transparency. This does not always mean better public engagement however, implicit in the terminology, as we shall see, there is a certain scientific hegemony within society. Society, in the main, trusts scientists regarding knowledge, as much as it trusts most technology.

Where does Public Participation Happen? Constructing the Public in the Context of Irish Science, Technology and Innovation

Strategic science communication, traditionally, was a one-way affair, science disseminated from an expert, without distortion to 'the public' via media (Hilgartner 1990). This dissemination model requires little feedback, and practically no critique. In some ways, this model still persists in Ireland. In late 1990s, early 2000s Ireland, with the emergence of the Celtic Tiger, there was an Irish 'turn to science'(Trench 2009) , starting with the Tierney Report (Ireland, Science, Technology and Innovation Advisory Council 1995)and the White Paper on STI White Paper (Ireland, Department of Commerce, Science, and Technology 1996) of the 1990s, a policy report that led to the setting up of Irish Council of Science Technology and Innovation (ICSTI, now ACSTI) .There then followed a ramping up of investment , not just of nanotechnologies, but of ICT and biosciences through the Programme for Research in Third Level Institutions (PRTLI).

As this model was embedded in an educational-knowledge economy-policy nexus, the 'education and outreach' allocation of funding was invested in increasing scientific awareness among second level students, in particular in often quite promotional activities, allied with an economic argument for emerging technologies, with the aspiration to also recruit future engineers. This aspiration still exists, as interest in science, technology, engineering and maths (STEM) secondary and higher education subjects, as well as literacy levels, decreases in this part of the world (Shiel *et al.* 2010). The objective of the investments made by the education-economy-policy nexus with EU support- would seem to have failed. Still, there have been many relatively large scale institutions and events created in the education and outreach arena which fulfil a valuable civic, as well as technological and economic, role, such as NanoNet Ireland, the Science Foundation Ireland-funded Centres for Science, Engineering and Technology (CSETs), and the Nano, Science and Engineers' Week events, all culminating in this year's ESOF Dublin City of Science 2012. But it could be argued that this continued emphasis on young people creates a kind of dialogue barrier, as topics such as nanotechnology become pedagogic rather than dialogic, an explanation of concepts in a top-down model. The City of Science emphasis on dialogue could be more accurately conceived as the start of a new conversation between science and society given the types of programmes organised - theatre, workshops and arts installations - a dialogue between traditions, not necessarily diverse publics. Another barrier for dialogue is the reduced risk discourse in media for science, technology and society generally, and specifically for nanotechnology. The stories of promise tend to be the only occurrence of nanotechnology in media coverage in Ireland (Murphy 2010), as it also tends to be abroad (Anderson *et al.* 2009).

The conditions for a reduced type of reflexivity in the institutions of science set up this non-dialogic, non-conflicting view of science in the public arena. The 'public' then is often in Irish policy-political culture – but also in global science communication strategy - constructed as a homogenously disinterested one, with young people in particular needing persuasion that science, maths and engineering is the way forward. Irish disposition toward science can be crudely characterised in attitudinal surveys, albeit with useful patterns (European Commission 2006c).

But why should scientists and policymakers be concerned with public opinion? As already alluded to, one reason is to ensure no repeat of what could be said to be 'the nuclear issue', which could also include GM scenarios, stalling industrial development. Genetically modified organisms have been the site of constant resistance against strategic science in Europe particularly, where there are accusations of PR softening up their market. Education and outreach would then be seen as a pre-emptive strike to remove public concerns and ignorance. In the US, the National Science Foundation allocates 6% of its funding to ethical, legal and social implications (ELSI). Another reason is: communication strategists are concerned about the general lack of engagement in science in Ireland. And this is a strong argument. For a nation that has had brilliant scientists – William Rowan Hamilton, Robert Boyle, Jocelyn Bell Burnell to name a few - and have embraced science both politically (politics with capital 'P', in that there is Government investment and promotion) and ontologically (we accept what we see and read about discoveries and phenomena), we do not, paradoxically, have a scientific culture. Boyle, in particular, was a dialogic scientist – not that he may have known it as described here – but he performed his science, out in the open, to his public, to convince and persuade that his empirical work was a description of scientific phenomena (Schaffer and Shapin 1989) (animals died during his vacuum pump demonstrations, so it is safe to assume we will not be repeating that level of intensity of public engagement today!).

Today however, this 'ELSI' strategy fits into an emerging discourse of public engagement in what can be broadly called socio-technical issues, meaning the social and cultural implications and dependencies of technologies (Schot and Rip 1997). But this strategy follows what is often called a 'deficit model' (Miller and Gregory 1998), assuming a knowledge gap to be filled only, revealing an outmoded idea of 'knowledge', and a perceived 'public' that is non-expert, with a negative relationship with knowledge. Although concerned with public attitudes, Chris Toumey (2011) demonstrates this traditional 'poling' view of public opinion in recent ongoing concerns about public opinion. But behind this, although 'knowledge' is the key construction it is seen as a deficit, although the intentions may be noble.

This construction of the public too easily separates science from politics. And this is the common mistake – the assumption that such a separation is possible. Many scholars such as Brian Wynne and Alan Irwin, as well as high level science policy reports (Felt *et al.* 2007) – and more radically, Michel Callon (1986) and Bruno Latour (2004) – have demonstrated how that intuitive separation of 'science' and 'politics' or 'knowledge' from 'opinion' is doomed to failure. In this separation, it becomes easy to construct a public in terms of a range of 'knowledge' and 'attitudes', somewhat outside the reflexive system, rather than social phenomena created by institutional systems themselves (even political polling has its issues in this regard). When publics (we therefore refer to 'publics' not 'public) are constructed in this way, it is seen that for general issues of science and society (including nanotechnology) there is a lack of engagement, a removal from discourse.

Technoscience and the Local

Technology, Local Opinion and Politics
To bring matters closer to home, let us examine how nanotechnology can be a matter of concern to a local community, even where the word may have little currency. We have already mentioned the low occurrence of 'risk talk' in media for science, technology and society also found for nanotechnology (Anderson *et al.* 2009). In environmental issues, local activism – where science reaches a zenith as a matter of concern – is unfairly characterised as NIMBY-ism. Again, the socio-technical nature of science/politics can be described by Beck (1992) and Giddens (1991) in their descriptions of sub-politics, action beneath the surface level, at a remove from media preoccupation with 'capital P' politics. There is a growing backlash fuelled by economic and political disillusionment and driven by civil society in Ireland. Examples include the *Occupy* movements, *Claiming Our Future, Galway 2040, Social Justice Ireland,* and for environmental issues, *Shell to Sea, Cork*

Harbour Alliance for a Safe Environment (CHASE) and, more recently, *Good Energies Alliance Ireland*, a collaborative of campaigners against shale gas hydraulic fracturing, or fracking, the latest socio-technical controversy in Ireland. As Brian Wynne skilfully demonstrated in his study of 'lay knowledge', the subjective of jobs and livelihoods versus fears of corporatist bullying versus scientific rationality are all part of a web of opinion in various local public arenas where there are socio-technical disputes (Wynne 2005). While science as knowledge, politics as "mere" opinion, Wynne challenges us to look to new definitions. For nanotechnology, while the risk discourse is practically absent (due to lack of current knowledge), particular questions about technology and industry in the real world need to be addressed in post-troika Ireland. Can there be real jobs in a nano-economy? What are the understandings of nanotechnology within society and local culture? These are the kind of questions the more community-engaged dialogue models discussed in the next section raise.

Community Engagement with Science: An Irish Citizen Jury for Nanotechnology

As already discussed, research and development in nanotechnologies and other convergent future and emerging technologies increased substantially in developed economies - and so-called BRIC and Asian countries - at the same as an increase in emphasis in dialogic potential in science communication fields, at least notionally. I say notionally, as public engagement exercises such as the *GM Nation* initiative in the UK during Gordon Brown's Labour Government was accused of using deliberative methodologies, such as focus groups, to gather social intelligence rather than address real public concerns (Gaskell *et al.* 2003). The EPA project reported in this chapter attempted to investigate this 'new breed' of science dialogue in an Irish context. The types of public engagement activity used in this study included secondary school visits, an installation in the Science Gallery with supporting online forum, the Alchemist Café - a *café scientifique* with an Irish flavour - and focus groups (newly created, open invitation and pre-existing groups) (see Murphy 2010 for the full research). The four categories used as evaluation criteria in the research, based on guidelines developed by the OECD on nanotechnology public engagement (Gavelin *et al.* 2007; OECD Directorate for Science, Technology and Industry Committee for Science and Technological Policy 2008), were:

- Emphasis on dialogue;
- Range of participation;
- Depth of issue or topic engagement;
- Impact.

In the evaluation, each public dialogue model had different 'scores' across the criteria. For example, the open invitation focus groups were high on depth of scientific/ issue engagement, but lower on range of participation, owing to low numbers. The Science Gallery installation had many visitors, so was high in range of participation and also potential impact due to large numbers, but lower on issue depth.

We will focus here on the citizens' jury activity, given its potential for high emphasis on dialogue and issue depth, and reflect on what impact it could have, specifically for science policy. Citizen juries are a type of public participation process whereby members of the public, up to 25 in number, are invited to make informed decisions as part of a 'jury' on an issue – in this case future and emerging technologies - based on key expert presentations, or 'witnesses.' The jury participants are offered the opportunity to listen, cross-examine and deliberate. The process has a 'charge', much like a debate motion, in which the facilitator/ judge and the jury must decide for or against the issue, but in contrast to a criminal trial, the verdict can contain more nuanced steps toward resolution, rather than a straightforward 'guilty' or innocent'. The citizen jury model has been successful in the Netherlands and Denmark but also in other Western countries, most successfully resolving issues or developing ideas as solutions where solutions can exist for particular community issues, such as criminality or anti-social behaviour. A citizens' jury on this latter issue was carried out in 2003 (Breeze 2003).

For nanotechnology, there are some precedents, most notably Nanojury UK organised by Tom Wakeford and colleagues at, PEALS, Newcastle University (Nanojury 2005). This was an intriguing process, as it contained parallel tracks – a 'top down' approach where the organisers – university researchers, but also included Greenpeace - set the terms for debate on nanotechnology with a corresponding 'bottom-up' track where the participants were asked to organise their own community-based topic. However, Singh (2005) who was on the facilitator team, urges us to be cautious, stating that the main reasons that the UK Nanojury was less than successful was 1) more time was required to deepen the bottom-up process rather than closing off discourse with the top-down process and 2) the issue of balancing participant expectations with real policy change. This of course means increased investment of time and money. Nonetheless, with these challenges, it was decided to run a small-scale Irish version as part of an EPA-funded pilot in DCU on May 16th 2009, with contributors from North Dublin local development agencies as jurors. The jury numbered six in total, with not all being able to remain for the almost full-day event. This is one challenge with such a dialogue model, requiring significant commitments from over-stretched community workers. A healthcare ethicist, a principal investigator in nanoscience research and a deliberative democracy expert were the 'witnesses', all from DCU, and facilitated by a DCU science communication team. The charge was: 'Does small science pose big problems for public policy?'

The short verdict returned by the jurors was 'yes'; however, as with citizen jury convention, there was a more detailed response to the charge. The verdict read that societal issues may not be significantly different for nanotechnology than they were for other big technologies to which society has adapted in the past. The charge outlined questions that nanotechnology raises for society:

- *Policy:* Will policymakers and publics acknowledge the local/global issues regarding the regulation, control and consumption of nanotechnologies? What is the Government position on nanotechnology? Who are the stakeholders? Are there community-based stakeholders? Does policy drive innovation or vice versa?
- *Risk:* Nanotechnology may bring profound changes, but society will adapt. While there was no consensus (and we need not expect consensus in these type of deliberative models), the majority felt that new pervasive technologies always have risks and benefits. Social and ethical risks were seen to be the more visible risks, rather than health or environmental ones;
- *Ethics/ inequity of knowledge domains:* Nanotechnology knowledge might never reach the disenfranchised, or those in disadvantaged areas, or their involvement - in research and development - would be minimal. There was a feeling that publics may be largely unaware of nanotechnology developments.
- *Trust:* It was felt by the jury that citizens will always raise the issue of trust – who is telling me this technological information? And

what do expert governance structures know that we (non-experts) need to know?

Science Policy: Public Response and Emerging Technologies as Political Action

The citizen jury verdict also stated that policy-makers were the key people in terms of setting the agenda for science in industry and the education system. There were concerns for implications for students in disadvantaged areas regarding access to nanotechnology knowledge for the future. It was clear to the jury that nanotechnology, as with many other so-called 'disruptive technologies,' has many interconnecting implications for science policy in Ireland which goes beyond science and technology. Policymakers, stakeholders and publics, the jurors stated, may tend to 'exist in bubbles' regarding these issues, but is it clear that nanotechnology has both local and global implications. It was important then to have policymakers represented at the next jury event, it was said. The key is to have science policy change as an intended outcome of the process. In this community-based approach, it was also informative to witness how local practical problems of education, jobs training or 'up-skilling' were integrated with ethereal and abstract debates in nano-science discourses, public contribution and policy buy-in.

There are other examples where nano-scale research and related technologies contain flatter democratic processes. The 'science shop' movement beginning to have an elevated status in University College Cork, Dublin Institute of Technology and DCU. In the science shop model, the research question emerges from the local community, rather than the techno-scientific community of higher education institutions (an example in which DCU is currently involved is the PERARES project, where networks and communities across Europe debate online about potential nano futures, through the organising of frames of energy or cancer treatment). Going further, there are also participatory design concepts, in the sense of common public and expert involvement, perhaps with different purposes (Guston and Sarewitz 2002). The vision is for community engagement with publics having direct ownership to how a technology develops, such as smart meters or photovoltaics [22] , while also responding to the debates about nanotechnology and energy in the outside world.

Conclusion

Nanotechnology is part of a discourse of technoscience from which we cannot escape nor do we necessarily need to. But it is a multi-pathway area of discourse where dialogical action already happens, between disciplines, institutions and various media. So why is the dialogue not more equitable? Ireland has a lack of engagement with socio-technical issues and an elite discourse that rarely allows dissent. There is an absence of 'risk talk' in public discourse about science, technology and society, whatever about debates within science itself about theories or processes. There are many global debates about science governance, ethics and funding. Citizens juries or panels are one solution for community-based fora where representations overlap between democratic principles and effective science communication, while avoiding the 'Phantom Public' temptation (Lippman 1993 [1927]), that is, constructing a homogenous public that does not exist, while at the same time paying attention only to scientific literacy. We must, of course, be careful. Foreign models have been applied to an Irish situation many times in the past, not always unsuccessfully. We cannot push engagement, and we must see if Irish people really connect with the narrative of Ireland as a world-class scientific island. However, we have still a way to go. Despite the dialogue planned for the City of Science nobody was asked to be critical of science, at its most fundamental. Paradoxically, the abstract was dealt with through film, art and theatre, the epistemological questions were addressed, but not the everyday practice.

The collapse of the Irish economy within the continuing European financial, and political crisis has prompted many to cry out for a new republic, where power structures are called to account or, if necessary, built anew. The banking and wider economic systems are included in this but as previously described, the governance of science is just such a power structure. The current Government insists that there are plans for citizens' assemblies. I would argue such a new imagining of a republic would place more emphasis on a democratic, responsible

---

[22] Photovoltaics is a method of generating electrical power by converting solar radiation into direct current electricity using semiconductors that exhibit the photovoltaic effect.

governance of science. What would 'responsible governance' mean? It would mean knowledge equity and social sustainability are framed equally within economic rationale and the technological development of a process or product. The dialogic element for a public emerging technology, in the case of nanotechnology, is a concentrated effort to employ various methodologies that allow publics to have a conversation with those who control the technologies, on an equal footing, not as a means just to 'learn from the experts'. There would be a middle ground of action, pockets of practice, where beliefs are not necessarily the issue – for example, dealing with immediate energy issues, photovoltaics, contributing to local or global problems as actors, with ownership of an issue, removing an immediate threat. In a modest way, even reporting here, in this book chapter, and subsequent policy reports there is some dissemination to stakeholders. These represent small steps to impact on science policy, connecting with the emergence of responsible innovation narrative (Murphy 2010)

Nanotechnology does promise much. But for Irish society, we are seeing many different futures presented before us, and the future we choose must be more inclusive than what has gone before. The lack of real public engagement in science has not been given the same level of attention as in other domains, but for emerging science and technologies and science governance, this inclusivity and flattening of power is just as important.

CHAPTER 10
PARTICIPATING IN POPULARISING POLICY ALTERNATIVES: A CASE STUDY OF *CLAIMING OUR FUTURE*

Mary P. Murphy

Introduction

This chapter examines the challenge Irish civil society faces in participating in political debate about real and credible alternatives. The first section explores theoretical concepts that assist an analysis of state and civil society relations and then briefly maps the obstacles to Irish civil society groups who want to promote alternative macro policy demands. The second section is a case study of *Claiming Our Future* which charts the experience of one sectors attempt to break free of sectoral boundaries and work with other sectors to set an agenda for alternative policy debate. The third section is the author's subjective analysis of this experience of working collectively to reshape the culture and public sphere within which Irish civil society engages in policy debate. The paper concludes by asking whether this has led to greater agenda setting power and greater capacity to increase the range of policy alternatives being discussed.

Some theoretical frames

This chapter is aligned with Edward's (2005) vision of civil society as creative, collective, values-based action that is capable of imagining alternatives. This understanding draws on Habermasian understandings of the public sphere as a place of deliberation, the importance of rich associational life and the importance of normative values which aim for a good society. This definition of civil society was used in Ireland by the Carnegie Inquiry into Civil Society (2007) and is consistent with Powell's (2007) argument for a 'social left'. The stress on alternative ideas is important. Without a struggle of ideas political debate only focuses on what can be done within conventional institutions. Politics becomes managerial and fails to collectively maximise societal capacity to reach the full experience of humanity and development. Engagement of the electorate in ideational debate requires rich forms of participatory democracy and what Unger (2011) calls a 'high energy democracy'.

A core debate within social sciences concerns the tension between structure and agency. The state provides a significant part of the 'institutional landscape within which political actors must negotiate' and the 'back drop to political conflict, contestation and change' (Hay, Lister and Marsh 2006: 11). This paper identifies a process of 'state capture' where the state, through its institutions, places macro and micro practical and cultural boundaries on different actors' capacity to participate in the policy process, and how they participate in debate about change. Such institutions, or rules of the game, generally work to reinforce the status quo and a narrow range of policy alternatives. A second theoretical perspective that counterbalances the first is that people have agency and power to change their world. Polanyi describes how, when society is threatened by crisis, a dialectical 'double movement' from an 'active society' works as a transformative agent to re-embed an unsustainable commodified economy so that it again meets the needs of society (Burawoy 2003). This is consistent with Gramsci's understanding of the role of civil society, both legitimating ruling hegemony but also producing alternative hegemonies.

Acheson *et al.* (2004: 197) argue the Irish state plays a key role 'in structuring the civic space in which voluntary action occurs' and that 'interaction of state drivers with cultural and ideological forces' shapes voluntary action and development. The question arises of how Irish state institutions have historically impacted on the shape of Irish civil society and its capacity to develop debate about alternatives. Irish civil society has been described by the late Peter Mair (2010) as stagnant and passive; it can be seen as a 'low energy democracy'. Political science literature often refers to Ireland's four C's of Catholicism, Centralisation, Clientalism and Corporatism, these impacted on the nature of Irish civil society and its orientation to political imagery. Participation in public discourse is limited to a pragmatic and anti-intellectual political sphere, where consensus was valued and conflict and dissent resisted (Kirby and Murphy 2009, 2011). This was reinforced by the nature of elite power and group think, the nature of the education and academy as well as the nature of the Irish media. In effect Irish civil society was characterized by an absence of overt ideology, conflict, ideas and debate about alternatives (Kirby and Murphy 2009).

Irish civil society is in some respects a prisoner of a form of populist democracy where the culture promotes clientalistic and 'cordial' political relations and where civil society groups who have an interest in political and distributional debate are encouraged into small, divided sectors. Corporatism promotes a pragmatic and 'problem solving' approach and a consensual process where the rules of the game require agreement to shared understanding and a commitment to leaving alternative perspectives outside the processes, thus continuing a well established culture of Irish anti-intellectualism (Lee 1989). It is not surprising, therefore, that few Irish responses to the crisis have managed to capture public debate about a different or alternative approach to understanding and resolving the crisis.

Despite the populist rhetoric of unity, there was in practice a very fragmented and divided civil society. Historically shaped into 'silos' or discrete sectors (women, disability, unions, environment, farming etc), these pursue sectional interests and are less likely to engage in macro policy debate, an orientation reinforced by two decades of embracing partnership with the state. Some of these sub groups were deemed more deserving than the other, this militated against solidarity. As groups became reliant on statutory funding schemes, civil society became increasingly marked by an intense sectoral fragmentation (Cox 2010).

Macro distributional debate and imagination is limited when civil society is preoccupied with and organised around single issue micro agendas. A catch 22 exists. It is easier to mobilise civil society if people believe an alternative is possible, but without mobilisation it is difficult to generate political debate to develop alternatives. Even in the context of significant anger at the response to crisis there is a poverty of ambition and imagination about alternatives in Ireland. This rest of this paper explores a recent attempt to develop a cross sectoral alliance to promote progressive alternatives. It begins pre crisis in 2006 and traces the process to March 2012.

The evolution of Claiming Our Future

In 2006, before the present crisis had manifested itself, this author was approached to work with Community Platform (CP)[23], a network of 28

---

[23]Organisations currently in the Community Platform are: ATD 4th World, Age Action Ireland, Community Action Network, Community Workers Co-operative, Cairde,

national networks and organisations within the Community & Voluntary sector working to address poverty, social exclusion and inequality. The CP had since 1996 acted as a mechanism to negotiate and organise the participation and involvement of the sector as a social partner in decision-making arenas at a national level. Part of their motivation in commissioning this work was an awareness of the need to engage in fresh thinking about alternative development models, that tweaking the dominant model was less and less likely to realize progressive change and more and more likely to contribute towards legitimizing the status quo. It's conscious decision to step outside the frame and 'smothering embrace' of social partnership reflected an analysis about the need to create a different space and new tools to think about alternatives. The process produced *A better Ireland is possible* (Kirby and Murphy 2008), a tool through which member organisations could engage in debate about alternatives, share a common analysis and:

> ... *contribute to the emerging debate on the nature of Irish society and democracy, which moves beyond current realities to foster genuinely creative responses to new and intransigent socio-economic challenges..... in a mature democracy - one that values pluralism, diversity and governance - everyone has the right to participate in generating an alternative vision, and everyone shares the responsibility in ensuring we succeed (Kirby and Murphy 2008: 1).*

Over this time period, six national anti-poverty networks [24] commissioned an independent researcher to review a series of legislative funding and institutional changes to state supports for the community and voluntary sector. They were responding to a number

European Anti-Poverty Network (EAPN) Ireland, Gay and Lesbian Equality Network, Immigrant Council of Ireland, Irish Association of Older People, Irish National Organisation of the Unemployed, Irish Penal Reform Trust, Irish Refugee Council, Irish Rural Link, Irish Traveller Movement, Migrant Rights Centre Ireland, National Adult Literacy Agency, National Network of Women's Refuges and Support Services, National Traveller Women's Forum, National Women's Council of Ireland, Older Women's Network, OPEN, Pavee Point, Rape Crisis Network Ireland, Simon Communities of Ireland, Threshold, Voluntary Drug Treatment Network, Vincentian Partnership for Justice, and Women's Aid.

[24] Community Workers Co-operative, European Anti-Poverty Network (EAPN) Ireland, Irish National Organisation of the Unemployed, Irish Traveller Movement, Migrant Rights Centre Ireland, National Traveller Women's Forum, National Women's Council of Ireland, OPEN and Pavee Point.

of government cutbacks and policy changes that had caused serious realignments in the community development programme, local development programme and charity legislation. There were suspicions that the state was consciously reshaping its relationship with that sector, and that it was necessary to gain a more critical understanding of the relationship between the state and civil society. *No Strings Attached* (Harvey 2009a: 1) confirmed what many suspected, the state was actively curtailing the space and activities of the community and voluntary sector and pushing it away from community development and towards service delivery. A launch of this report stimulated significant and ongoing reflection on the relationship between the state and civil society, a launch conference attended by almost 200 people collectively reflected on the changing nature of Irish state-civil society relations.

Following this launch, those who commissioned the report met informally to develop their reflection on this growing tension in the relationship between the community sector and the state and what this meant for participative democracy.[25] That these individuals informally called themselves the 'Gunpowder Plot' reflected the mood at the time. Over a period of months, this network evolved by members extending personal invitations to other activists considered leaders in communities considering these tensions. At this stage, September 2008, this author was invited to work facilitating this group of approximately 20 people to reflect on how they could usefully work together. This time period overlapped with Obama's 2008 presidential campaign and reflecting this time of hope and optimism the group called themselves *Is Feidir Linn* (IFL). Reflecting Anne Marie Smith (1998: 7) "that political struggle does nevertheless depend in part on the ability to imagine alternative worlds" they set themselves the task of imagining an alternative Ireland and contributing to the emergence of a social movement to create and advance this alternative Ireland. This ambitious challenge was progressed at a well-attended conference in June 2009 where IFL launched *'Shaping our Future'* (IFL 2009), an initial sketch of a balanced model of development. This marked the beginning of an attempt to break free of silos and develop a broad alliance for an alternative. IFL spent the following six months on a deliberate exercise

---

[25] It is worth noting in parallel to this, research funded by Atlantic Philanthropies was also examining the impact of state policy on advocacy work (Harvey 2009b).

talking, listening and building trust with other sectors in Irish civil society[26]. The aim of the dialogue was to build a wider cross-sectoral mobilization of those who want a more equitable, sustainable and thriving Ireland. IFL identified and targeted their dialogue up to ten 'sectors', these included faith, environmental, youth, trade union, development, the Trotsky Irish left and the libertarian Irish left, democracy campaigners, culture and arts groups and academic communities. While reaction was mixed, the dialogue was generally well received and IFL felt encouraged to take the next step.

In January 2010, IFL began a dialogue with the Irish Congress of Trade Unions, some organisations from the Environmental movement, the Community Platform, TASC and Social Justice Ireland.[27] All had published visions of alternatives, none were pursuing any electoral strategy to promote their vision of alternatives and all had indicated an eagerness to collaborate in some form to promote the need for alternatives. These six agreed to explore the potential for a wider civil society cooperation and coordination around the search and demand for an alternative to the current response to economic recession. This process identified shared barriers to building any impetus for change and putting an alternative analysis into the public domain. Common barriers included the tendency to work in silos, the difficulty in breaking through to mainstream media and linking national work to local members or groups. A sense emerged through talking, listening, trust building, sharing ideas, reflecting on strategies and looking to international experiences that three key principles could help maximise debate about and support for alternatives – that the work should be *society led*, in other words it should not be vulnerable to being controlled by the state, it should seek to create a state free public sphere. This should be *cross-sectoral* bringing together groups who previously worked in their own narrow silos. The methods used needed to *enable national and local mobilisation,* debate about alternatives needed to be relevant to people's lives.

The next step was to identify ways to build consensus, momentum, solidarity and alliances among those interested in this vision and these

---

[27] There remained within IFL a group of people motivated to address the original focus in Harvey (2009a) which focused on the impact of government cuts and institutional changes on the community and voluntary sector and participative democracy.

goals, with a view to working towards an inclusive, equal and sustainable Ireland. Three possible strategies emerged:

- To develop a common narrative (to that end all the different visions of alternatives were collated into a single *choices document);*
- A media campaign where press officers in the various networks would work to co-ordinate and maximise the synergy around press releases;
- A public event to mobilise support and popularise the idea that alternatives were possible. Inspired in part by public events and responses to the crisis in Iceland *(the Anthill).*

A public deliberative event was planned in the belief that civil society has a vital contribution to make in identifying and progressing new policy choices. An ambitious event was planned to provide an opportunity to discuss and deliberate on values, the implications of these values for new policy choices and to identify ways of cooperating and coordinating to advance these values and policy choices. Local meetings and activities were held throughout the country in the lead up to the event, demand significantly exceeded capacity and on the day over 1300 booked in, 100 trained facilitators volunteered, €60,000 was raised from philanthropies and unions, office space, book keeping, information technology and event management skills were all volunteered. There was extensive use of social media; use of deliberative dialogue on the website was facilitated through free deliberative software. There was significant media and public interest in this deliberative event in the Industries Hall of the RDS in Dublin City on 30th October 2010.

This gathering used participative software influenced by the de Borda Institute to consensually agree a number of priority values (equality for all, environmental sustainability, accountability from those in power, participation by people in decision making that impacts on them, solidarity between all sectors of society and a sustainable alternative to our boom-and-bust economy). These values were then reflected in six agreed priority policy agendas (a more equal society, change in the way we govern ourselves, decent and sustainable jobs, radical reform of the banking system, and renewal of our public services). Following this model subsequent national *ideas events* were held to explore Income Inequality (in Galway in May 2011) and

Economy for Society (in Cork in November 5th 2011) and Reinventing Democracy (in Dublin May 2012).

While COF has subsequently struggled to capture the sense of scale or energy of that day, it has managed to maintain a healthy infrastructure of groups and networks and supporters who worked so well to put the day together. While the infrastructure is relatively fluid, there are some stabilisers. As well as 7,000 who have registered on its web site it has loose networks in local areas country wide and three thematic working groups Income Inequality, Economy for Society, Democracy. A mobilisation group plan action campaigns. This is coordinated through monthly meetings. Campaigns to date included a 2010 high profile campaign to restore the minimum wage, a 2011 gender quota campaign and a 2011 wealth tax campaign. An assembly of COF activists meets twice a year. The focus on alternatives has been progressed, through a core Plan B political economy campaign which runs over 2012-2013.

The good the bad and the ugly

It is not yet clear what COF is. While the intention is to be a fluid social movement of individuals and groups, a core strength is often its capacity to utilize the good will of sympathetic organisations. A strategy document sets out a plan to the end of 2013. The movement remains voluntary, but has secured basic funding of €50,000 p.a. (2012-2014) from the Joseph Rowntree Trust. It has also secured office space and a full-time voluntary administrator, who coordinates a small number of interns to provide administrative, social media and networking support. There have been clear networking and collaborative opportunities between groups in COF and also between COF and other progressive networks for change. All of this strengthens solidarity a key objective of COF.

Beyond agreeing rhetorical sound bites, there are significant challenges in maintaining a broad coalition of people who use different language and have different starting points in where they approach debate about alternatives. The focus of COF has been to deliberate, but not to force, a consensus on such issues. From its inception COF did successfully capture public imagination, the following lines from the *Changing Ireland* editorial capture a sense of the initial energy at RDS in Dublin October 2010:

There have been other think-tank conferences, but this one was different because it captured the public imagination. It promises to be real, to inspire people to take action and to be locally rooted. Everyone from business people to barristers to homeless people and activists were at the event....... It has the potential to become a vehicle for replacing public fear with a sense of national purpose, destiny and collective action. While there is a danger it could dwindle to become another talking shop, a comfort-blanket for people on the left, people are determined that won't happen...... In a positive sign, many old hands and sceptics have put caution aside and embraced the work. There is a hunger for new ideas and a push for taking action that can lead to positive change (2010: 1).

While the initial rush of enthusiasm has faded there still remains a positive groundswell of support for the original intentions of *Claiming Our Future* and its analysis. Many welcomed the initiative, the risk taking and the hard work. For many local activists, the public space and to some degree the hope and optimism created by COF fills a vacuum and allows people make national relevance of their local work. A significant shortcoming however was the inability to seize the moment to establish and build on the energy created on October 30th 2010 and to have immediate follow on, in terms of keeping people involved and active.

There is always the challenge of maintaining a cross-sectoral space. There are more activists from the community sector than the environmental, trade union and other sectors. While these strong working relationships have been advantageous, they also represent a fault line as there is a danger of being self-reinforcing as the language, culture and work patterns of one sector can dominate; a space can appear exclusive and there is the risk of clique formation (perceived or real). While its strategic plan explicitly distances it from electoral politics COF has been mistakenly perceived as a front for various political parties (occasionally Sinn Féin, more often the Labour Party) and also as a new political party (such accusations may sometimes be mischievous). It is also vulnerable to perceptions that individuals may be promoting their own agendas. There does need to be a conscious effort to circulate voices and leadership so no one voice dominates a movement but it is also true that much of what has been achieved has been down to individual leadership.

There have been accusations of idealism and utopianism, charges have been made of gullibility and naivety 'state funded radicals' making imaginary castles (Fitzgibbon 2010). The reader will have their own judgement but for many activists, the alternative of doing nothing is not an option. While people of course have a right to be sceptical, a certain amount of idealism and utopianism is inevitable if the objective is stretching the boundaries of the political imaginary. There is a real tension in the movement having short-term relevance to the needs of the activists on the ground working and living in difficult circumstances and the vaguer long-term objective of promoting policy alternatives and political imagination[28]. So too, there is a tension in being relevant and responding to demands for immediate responses to issues and duplicating the work of existing single issue campaigning groups focused on those issues. While the focus has been on solidarity with other campaigns, there is considerable demand to initiate or, more directly, support specific campaigns.

Conclusion

It is difficult to assess whether this experience has to date contributed to developing a greater public sphere and/or increased the range of policy alternatives being discussed. There are no established indicators of success, and it is still early days, but there has been some public sphere and media success.

The focus on concern for urgent debate about alternative futures remains largely absent from mainstream party politics. The nature of Irish political discourse, coupled with media ownership, points away from a high-energy democracy. Debate about political alternatives is unlikely to happen from 'above'. If alternatives are likely to come 'from below' the challenge remains to nurture and cherish public spheres and civil society where citizens can deliberate and develop their political imagination (Smith 1998; Unger 2011). COF remains part of our collective challenge of creating public space to collectively imagine and argue for a better world.

Erik Olin Wright (2012a: 23) argues the best starting point for social transformation, 'is to do things now which put us in the best position to

---

[28] Indeed a similar debate about immediate relevance versus stretching boundaries of imagination about what is possible has happened in the context of the world wide Occupy Movement.

do more later'. He argues 'institutional pluralism of the destination suggests strategic pluralism in the practices of transformation' and this requires 'greater levels of respect and cooperation among different political traditions of anti-capitalism through understanding them as complementary rather than antagonistic' (2012: 14). Baker et al. (2004: 246) agree 'strategic pluralism is a strength not a weakness'. Claiming Our Future does not claim to be radical, it does claim to be progressive, this article has pondered its own strengths and weaknesses and its honest contribution to the struggle for a more equal and sustainable future.

CHAPTER 11
OCCUPYING DUBLIN / RIDING THE WAVE

Helena Sheehan

Another global wave of critique and resistance would come, I told myself and anyone who asked. For many years I watched and waited. Not passively, but actively, keeping alive the social memory of movements past, analysing the ever shifting shape of the global system and going into the streets to protest against many forms of exploitation. We no longer had the wind at our backs. Our numbers were small. Our voices were marginalised. Nevertheless we knew that the structural problems that had brought us on to the streets in the beginning had not been solved.

As boom led to bust, expropriation intensified by means we never imagined possible. The level of anger rose greatly, but activity not so much. The powerful were even more powerful and we were so powerless. Iceland, Greece, Tunisia, Egypt, Spain, Chile, etc, etc. Would it be everywhere but here? Here being a country that had plunged down in the world far more dramatically than most. Yet we beheld signs of Greek protesters saying 'We are not Ireland'. The shame of it. What would it take to get Irish people to act?

The trade union movement got 100,000 out on the streets of Dublin in November 2010 and everybody went home again. After beholding the indignant on the squares of the world in 2011, I thought that we had to get out and stay out. Then came Occupy Wall Street. I tweeted: "#OccupyIFSC. Up for it?" I wasn't the only one. It was in the air. During the first week of October, it got focused. There were already several actions planned for 8th October. There were several small groups planning to be at the Central Bank in Dame Street with a street theatre flavour: one going for 'pots and pans' and another for 'the shirt off our back'. Then #OccupyDublin and #OccupyDameStreet started trending on Twitter. On Facebook too we got liking and planning.

It was spreading like wildfire throughout the US and other countries and continents too. I got reports from Occupy Philadelphia, the place where my protesting began. A meeting to plan it that week attracted massive attendance, including many of my new left friends, veterans of many protests, greyer now but still going, along with many new to protest. The occupation started on 6th October and I was mesmerised by the livestream. I was fascinated by a general assembly where participants responded to the question 'Why are we protesting?' by telling their stories in the call-and-response of the mic check ritual. There was a sixties feeling sweeping over me. A Buffalo Springfield song came back to me. It went "There's something happening here. What it is ain't exactly clear." I found it on YouTube and posted it and it spread. It kept playing in my head. Of course, I knew there was a difference between *the* 60s and *my* 60s, but I was determined to be up for it.

All week I was on the social networks stirring it up. I do not believe in the idea of Facebook or Twitter revolutions, because the impetus comes from real social conditions and relations, but these technologies and networks greatly enhance the capacity to connect and to build social movements. I am especially aware of it for having organised for so many years before they existed. I put everything else on hold. I stopped writing a book in mid-chapter. This book is an attempt to synthesise autobiography with intellectual and social history. It would not do to stay home and write about struggles of the past as a reason for not engaging with the struggles of the present. This is still my time. My position as a professor *emerita* gave me a certain freedom of time and movement.

I met with a number of people planning for Occupy Dublin / Occupy Dame Street to start on 8th October as well as for the international day of solidarity on 15th October at Seomra Spraoi, an autonomous social centre in Dublin city centre. It reminded me of many spaces of the sixties. I met people I had been interacting with on Facebook and Twitter, but had never met face-to-face. I saw a lot of them in the coming days. This was the weekly assembly of Real Democracy Now, a group that had formed out the 15-M movement in Spain. They had asked me to speak at the event they were planning for 15th October. Those who had put the #OccupyDameStreet hashtag on Twitter and set up the Occupy Dame Street Facebook page were there, looking to RDN as experienced organisers, as they had been in the field for a few months already.

On 7th October, the US embassy in Dublin warned US citizens to avoid the area around Dame Street, because of anti-financial-sector protests. I posted this to Facebook, which led to some discussion of a paranoid nature. I revealed that the US embassy was following me on

Twitter. It meant that we were getting the word out there, which was what we wanted to do. At the same time, we wanted to project it as a peaceful communal gathering to address what was happening in the world and not a skirmish between testosterone-charged hoodies and cops.

On 8th October, I woke up with a great sense of excitement, not knowing quite what to expect, but hoping for a new momentum in our political scene. I arrived at the plaza in front of the Central Bank on Dame Street just after 2pm. There were many people I had never seen before, along with ones I met during the week and a few I knew for many years. Most people did not know each other. There were 300 or so. I look back on that day with fondness, because the atmosphere was so fresh and open, because all voices were equal, because there was such hope in the air.

I suggested that we use the mic check idea, as I had been so moved by watching it in Philadelphia via livestream. One by one people came forward. It was a powerful ritual, reinforcing attention and building cohesion. We told our stories and said why we were angry and why we weren't going to take it anymore. We served notice that we were organising to take back the world that had been taken away from us. There were also conversations, one-to-one or in small groups. There was a sense of vital bonds being forged.

After seven hours, I went home and slept in my own bed. I didn't camp overnight, as I didn't think it appropriate to my age. I had done so in my youth, especially in 1971, where we created a massive encampment in Washington DC, as a base for mass civil disobedience in response to the continuing war in Vietnam. As soon as I got in the door, I tuned in to the livestream of Occupy Philadelphia, where there was a march from City Hall to Independence Hall. A young black girl was speaking, while the assembled repeated her words. "I am homeless. I am homeless. I am hungry. I am hungry. My grandmother is sick and can't afford health care ..." It was powerful. Resistance had stepped up its tempo.

I returned on day two, a Sunday, which was a much quieter day. I participated in a smaller assembly and found it really frustrating. It was about defining what we were. Over and over in the next days, I heard things that made me cringe at the conceptual confusion that seemed to prevail: assertions that this was not a political movement, that it was neither right nor left, that participants were welcome as individuals, but had to leave their politics at the door. I tried to be patient, to argue that a person's political philosophy was something integral to his/her being and not something that could be left at the door, aside from the other absurdity of this constant injunction - the fact that we had no door! I invoked a conception of politics that was broader and deeper than party politics. We need to reclaim the polis, I contended. Some took the point, but others continued with the 'no politics' rhetoric regardless.

There was also a problem, especially when speaking to the media, about when a person could say 'we believe' as opposed to 'I believe'. 'I, the people', one tweeter wryly remarked. There were many personal opinions put forward as collective expressions, which I found really objectionable, especially the declarations of 'no politics here'. Someone from the Workers Party came along with some copies of the latest issue of *Look Left*, an attractive, intelligent, broad left magazine, to contribute to the library and was told 'no politics here'. However they were eventually accepted and hopefully read.

I understood and accepted the determination to create a movement with no affiliation to political parties and to resist entryism on the part of any existing political formations. However, discussions were dominated by an unhealthy emphasis on who / what to keep out rather than who / how to bring in support for this movement. There was an obsession with a ban on political and trade union banners and literature. There was fear of any organisation bringing its own agenda into this movement. In fact, *Real Democracy Now* brought its participants and its agenda into the Occupy movement in an entirely natural way. They involved themselves in all aspects of the occupation in a way that was hard working, enthusiastic and constructive. Another political grouping was the Workers Solidarity Movement, an anarchist group, whose members participated in an organic and constructive way, which no one found problematic.

From the beginning, in fact before the occupation actually started, much of such discussion was driven by hostility to the Socialist Workers Party. The immediate cause was that the SWP-driven *Enough* campaign had changed the date of their planned anti-IMF-ECB-EC march from the 8th to the 15th October, because of a change in the date of the troika visit and then asserted that their march was the Irish event in the international day of solidarity, whereas RDN had been organising to be the Irish event for that day for several months. Others involved in the occupation had some previous experience with the SWP and accused them of dominating broad organisations by monopolising membership lists and aggressively recruiting. These specific changes escalated to a way of talking about them as if they were sinister and evil, rather than being another force on the scene that was mobilising on the same issues. Any attempt by the SWP to relate to the occupation was seen as an attempt at infiltration. Perhaps, if they involved themselves more organically from the beginning and contributed to the camp and working groups, instead of coming along to assemblies when they wanted to argue specific positions, it might have been better, but then again it might also have increased the charges of infiltration. Some of those who became most hostile to the SWP had to ask initially 'What is the SWP?'

In the first week of the occupation, the working groups began to form. Eventually there were groups for food, security, construction, facilitation, solutions, outreach, media, talks and events. With every passing day, things became more organised and our lives moved to a new rhythm. There was a flurry of activity, especially on the plaza and the social networks. *The times they are a changin'* rang out in the night air. I loved the presence of this powerful song from my past in this present scenario. The music on the street during these months was one of the best things about the occupation. Christy Moore, Damien Dempsey, Liam Ó Maonlaí, Glen Hansard and many others sang at the site.

On day three, I went from ODS to the Mansion House for a memorial for Kader Asmal, who had lived and been active on the left in Ireland for many years before returning to South Africa, where he became a government minister. I felt an odd sense of dissonance in moving from one milieu to the other, where I was mixing with the next president of the nation, the mayor of the city, a minister in the government, some academics, even several Central Bank economists. ODS was barely a blip on their radar. Most all of them were left of centre, looking back in comfort at a spell of activism in the anti-apartheid movement of the past. When asked what I was doing these days, I mentioned ODS. Some showed an indulgent, but distant, interest, while others couldn't get away from me fast enough.

From day two on, the weight of my efforts went into organising a series of sixties-style teach-ins. We called it Occupy University. I hoped it would help to bring theoretical clarity and historical perspective to this project. We had two or three talks a day, all out in the open air on Dame Street, except in the heaviest rain, when we found nearby indoor venues. There was something bracing about doing it on the street and struggling with big ideas in the midst of noise of the buses, ambulances and fire engines and the interruptions of attention-seeking alcoholics and drug addicts. We also got passers-by, who stopped to listen and stayed to talk, while others tarried only long enough to tell us that we were wasting our time. We invited them to feel free to participate, but not to disrupt.

Many of our talks were about the global financial system: hedge schools versus hedge funds. We also concentrated on talks about previous social movements, as well as branching out to ideology and culture. We also had workshops on practical matters: writing, media, music, direct action. Those attending were of different ages, genders, races, occupations and, most importantly, different educational levels. There were professors and doctoral students along with people who had left school at an early age. Most speakers pitched their talks well to encompass this diversity. Speakers were academics, journalists, politicians, poets, bloggers, trade union officials, alternative media practitioners. Sometimes discussions stayed reasonably well focused and sometimes they went all over the place. There were conspiracy theorists and currency crazies and fluoride fanatics, who used the discussion of anyone else's talk as an platform to give their own talks. Mostly there was sincere sharing of knowledge and earnest interaction, pursued with a purity of purpose, all too absent in academe. In two months we organised 78 talks and workshops.

Sometimes we got so fired up about the nature of the whole global financial system and the revelation of local details of how flagrantly we were being robbed that we could hardly stand it. The Sunday morning when we listened and questioned blogger David Malone, while sheltering from the rain under the structure of the Central Bank, it was revealing, unbearable, poignant and funny all at once. Sometimes lecturers were asked questions that stopped them in their tracks. Andy Storey gave a lecture on the IMF and asserted that there had been zero rise in GDP in African countries 'assisted' by IMF programmes. An earnest young man was astounded and asked 'What? Even with Live Aid?' Actually he spoke for many Irish people, who believe that Bono and Bob had basically sorted out Africa. Sometimes people suggested measures to reform capitalism, such as a transaction tax, while other times people tried to imagine a future without capitalism. There was a lot of debate on the crisis in the eurozone. Terrence McDonough, professor of economics in Galway, made the strongest case for exiting the euro, whereas other economists cast doubt on this as a strategy.

Our system for booking talks was ad hoc, really rough and ready, but it worked. At least it worked until we had a minor crisis. At first the problem was being too tightly circumscribed. When I proposed a series of talks at the assembly on day three, everyone was all for giving us the go ahead. When I started elaborating further on topics and speakers and mentioned that Michael Taft was a trade union economist, the anti-trade-union reflex was triggered. Then one person, who was very assertive in week one and disappeared thereafter, suggested that we come back when we had the list more complete. It was looking as if every topic and every speaker would be argued at every assembly. I did not think that would be viable. It was logistically too awkward. A few days later we brought it up at an assembly again under the name of Occupy University and agreed to operate it autonomously. We set up a Facebook conversation as our mode of meeting, supplemented by texting to the site. I contacted radical academics, journalists and writers, whom I knew, as did a few others. Sometimes somebody appeared at the camp with a proposal or contacted us through the website. Not only was ODS a necessary venue for progressive tourists to visit and musicians to play, but an OU talk was the same for visiting progressive intellectuals, such as Patrick Bond and Michael Albert. Others who spoke included: Fintan O'Toole, Siobhan O'Donoghue, Harry Browne, Gavan Titley, Conor McCabe.

We never discussed criteria for speakers, because we assumed common understanding of the project. Until the name of Eamon Ryan appeared on our timetable. He was now leader of the Green Party, but had been a government minister, defeated in the election earlier in the year. He was a particularly arrogant exponent of the decisions that brought us to our knees. I was told that he would speak on 'energy, no politics', which I did not find acceptable. I introduced the session in a civil, but less than welcoming, way, asking participants to let him have his say, but indicating that all should be able to address the politics of energy as well as to air their grievances with the last government. The discussion veered from people losing their tempers at his very presence and walking away to engaging him in ideological debate to being honoured by his presence and trying to impress him. I was astounded at the latter, especially because I had been careful not to invite Richard Boyd Barrett of the SWP, who had been elected to Dáil Éireann in the recent election, or Alex Callinicos, when he was in town for the Marxism conference, as I thought it would inflame the situation at this stage. People who didn't want to be tainted by association with trade unions and left parties were gushing over a politician who voted for and justified what ODS was set up to protest.

We did invite academics, such as Marnie Holborow and Sinead Kennedy. We had a media workshop, given by Paula Geraghty, and a poetry anti-slam, organised by Dave Lordan, who also performed 'Living with the recession'. These were all well received, taken at face value, by participants who were unaware of their connection to the SWP. Paul Murphy MEP of the Socialist Party spoke at OU as well as an assembly. He wrote an article on politico.ie taking a constructive approach to the Occupy movement. Most received him well, although one wrote of left politicians having 'wet dreams of left unity' because of the Occupy movement.

Trade union officials tended to get a rough ride. When Mick O'Reilly spoke, a woman screeched at him demanding that he call a general strike immediately. When Sam Nolan gave a sketch of the history of trade unions in Ireland, it was our longest session, with many people coming and going. After several hours and darkness falling, a new wave of participants were asking questions that had been asked and answered two hours before that. One young woman ranted against trade unions from a position of utter ignorance.

I gave a talk myself the first week on the new left: remembering and reflecting. I told the story of the 1960s-1970s new left as it unfolded and as I experienced it, focusing on themes relevant to this new movement: redefining the political, naming the system, problems of leaderlessness, forms of resistance, prefigurative politics, relations of old left and new left, participatory democracy. When I used the phrase 'participatory democracy' in connection with the Port Huron Statement of 1962, I could see a look of shock on a few young faces, who thought it had just come into being with this movement.

I tried not to be an old know-it-all, who had been-there-done-that, but so many things being said and done did remind me of so much that had been said and done in the past and I did find myself saying so. At the same time, I did know that this historical conjuncture was unique. I felt that I had something specific to offer as a voice connecting past and present, as someone who could tell this story within the framework of a longer story.

The *Occupy* movement was clearly part of a narrative of the left, but it was broader than that. It encompassed elements who did not consider themselves left. The spectrum was wide, but tilted way to the left. The political philosophies most clearly in evidence were social democracy, Marxism and anarchism. Among those giving talks, Marxism was the strongest presence, although not in a doctrinaire, or even heavily sign-posted, way. Among those most actively seeking to form and articulate their political philosophies, particularly under the stimulus of new activism, anarchism seemed best to catch their mood and to impel them to develop further.

The issue of demands was a contentious one, particularly at OWS, although not so much at ODS. During the first week, there were four main demands formulated. These were: (1) an end to IMF/ECB control of the Irish economy (2) repudiation of private bank debt that had been socialised (3) national control over our oil and gas reserves (4) participatory democracy. Elsewhere in the Occupy movement there was reluctance to make demands, as demands imply acceptance of a system that the movement has set out to undermine or even overthrow. These were broad demands on which everyone could agree, but could not easily be conceded.

There was a dialectic between reform and revolution in play and a whole spectrum of positions on what the relation should be. Some came out of anger at 'corporate greed', which was not the same as a critique of capitalism, but for many it could be a step along the way to it. While the basic thrust of the movement was in the direction of a systemic critique of capitalism, there were some, here as elsewhere, who would be satisfied with a reformed capitalism and a return to national economic sovereignty. For those who were seeking more, the nature of the imagined alternative was clearly socialism for some, but something uncertain for many others. There were some who advocated a return to barter and Brehon law. The milieu was one where we could discuss alternative visions without having to come to agreement on a detailed programme or even a common political philosophy.

We had our first march on 15th October, the day of international solidarity. The ODS march fused with the RDN one already planned for that day. There was great sense of being part of a global wave.

There were occupations in nearly 1000 cities in 82 countries on 6 continents at that stage. Despite the complication of the *Enough* march, many people attended both and numbers were good (about 2000) and spirits were high. When we arrived at Dame Street, I spoke at the beginning of the assembly, as I had previously been asked to speak by RDN. I tried to combine reflection with rabble rousing, but the rabble needed little rousing. They were in fighting form. While recognising that this movement was about occupations and demands, I warned against reducing it to occupations and demands, especially against believing that this occupation in itself would lead to achievement of these demands. I argued that we needed to build a movement to engage in a complex, protracted and difficult struggle. I stressed that we were up against the most formidable force in the whole history of the world and that we did not really know how to unravel the structures of political and economic power that made it possible for the 1% to rule at the expense of the 99%. In other words, Marxist words, how to expropriate the expropriators. We do not really know how to do that now, which was a reason why we had to make the Occupy movement a site of study as well as a site of struggle. This was published in *Irish Left Review*.

The structures and rituals of the project came into shape: the camp, general assemblies, working groups, teach-ins, marches, musical and poetic performances, direct actions, conversations. Sometimes it all fell together in wondrous harmony, but discordant notes could be detected. There were problems at the core of the project that were bound to erupt into full-scale conflict, as they duly did.

One of these was the tension between camp and movement. From day two I felt that those who were free to camp had a disproportionate voice in defining and deciding what the movement would be. I wanted this to be a movement of those with jobs, kids, complications, lives that made it impossible to camp, but could find ways to participate according to their situations. Understandably it was those who were camping, many of whom were unemployed, who were available to do the media interviews, who could attend the general assemblies at 1pm and 6pm every day. At an early stage, there were no agendas available in advance and no minutes to check afterwards. Although I was there almost every day for 3 to 7 hours a day, I was not present when crucial decisions were made, such as the ban on party political and trade union banners and literature from the site as well as from all marches and activities of ODS on other sites. It was by no means obvious that trade unions and left parties wanted to rush in to be part of this and to bring their banners on our marches. The contradiction between the declarations of inclusiveness and practices of exclusiveness would continue and accentuate to the point of absurdity.

There were bound to be problems basing a movement in a camp, but there were also pluses. It was symbolically powerful to occupy a public space, especially there in the city centre, as a 24/7 visible challenge to the system, a 24/7 point of contact for people to come to participate in opposition to it.

It was not only about opposition. It was about forming new bonds of solidarity and experimenting in participatory democracy. It was about giving and receiving food, shelter, culture, knowledge and labour, liberated from the circuitry of commodification. There was strong sense of prefigurative politics, of building the new in the shell of the old, of being the change we wanted to see in the world. There were times when the plaza was alive with this sense of an alternative space. There was such a buzz to all that talk, music and activity on the street.

I was full of zeal for this idea in my new left days and subsequently saw our counterculture ebb away, but it left its mark, not only on me, but on the wider culture. I still believe in this approach in my older (and hopefully wiser) way. This determination to make the means compatible with the ends, which is important, also carries the danger of becoming obsessed with the means to the neglect of the ends. This made us turn in on our own identities, our own process, our own collectives, in the past in a way that sometimes diverted our energies or even subverted efforts to build a wider movement.

Some of those camping became obsessed with the camp and with an inflated image of themselves as the core of this movement. "I camp therefore I am" I said of them on one occasion, when I was frustrated by the camp narcissism, paraphrasing Descartes to ends he never intended. One habitually referred to himself and others in the camp as 'heroes of the revolution'. He constantly posted self-glorifying (and unattributed) quotations on Facebook about how a few people could change the world and hit back at anyone who did not give unconditional support as enemies. Some resented those who came for the talks and assemblies, but did not camp, questioning their right to have a say at assemblies. Some even resented those who were in working groups, who did much of the work of the movement and were around for long hours during the day, either at the camp itself or doing organising work elsewhere. On two occasions, Occupy University talks were interrupted to demand that those attending wash dishes or move tarps, although there were others hanging around who were available. I took it as an act of hostility and lost my temper the second time it happened. Some in the camp never attended talks and rarely attended assemblies and seemed vexed at them even happening. At the same time they felt free to come and to block when they got wind of proposals not to their liking and said to people, who worked and came consistently to assemblies, that they should camp if they wanted to be part of this movement and have their say.

From their point of view, they were outside in the cold, the rain and the dark when others were home asleep in their warm beds. They were vulnerable to the drunks, junkies, thieves and crazies on the city streets when others were secure in their homes. They were up all night on security duty while others arrived after a good night's sleep seeking interesting company and intellectual conversation. Money, laptops, mobile phones were stolen. Inappropriate sexual conduct had to be addressed. Knives were pulled. People got on each other's nerves. As with most occupations, the homeless came and found a higher standard of food, shelter, security and community than was their norm. At the same time, people often became homeless because of other problems, problems which a political encampment was not always equipped to solve or even cope.

I respected their efforts to stay there in difficult material conditions, especially those who got on with it and remembered the political purpose of it, but I found it hard to take the guilt tripping attitude of some of those who camped to those who didn't camp. At one assembly I asked: 'Do you want to build a camp or do you want to build a movement?' I believed that a camp obsession, even narcissism, was subverting the attempt to build a movement. What kind of movement could it be if it repelled people who work, people with obligations and problems that prevent them from camping? It had to be a movement open to people to contribute as they were able. It had to be a movement that those people could be part of defining. Division of labour was bound to be a fraught issue and it impacted on all the working groups and other aspects of the project. Allowing for life situations and resulting availability, I was astonished at how much some people with complicated lives gave to the effort and disappointed at how little others with fewer complications stepped up to do.

The assertion of the priority of the camp put people off. Some went away. I was tempted to do so, but stayed, even if I was often angry and alienated. I sometimes found myself speaking of ODS as 'they' rather than 'we', but I still struggled to say 'we'. Even if I wasn't camping, I had made a drastic change in the rhythm of my life. It was a 24/7 project and I gave myself to it fully. Even when I was home, I was at the computer giving an account of it, trying to raise support for it, finding out what was going on globally. It was always in my head. When I went to sleep at night, I was dreaming about it. It seemed the biggest thing that was happening in the world in the way of resistance to the terrible forces ranged against us. Despite being obsessively orderly, I let housework go. I found it difficult to keep up with my e-mail. I stayed up far later at night than was my habit, but got up at the early hour as was my custom. I was stressed, exhausted and irritable at times.

There were ongoing tensions about trade unions and political parties, specifically those of the left. Things that were said made me furious. Basically there was a vociferous element, who declared over and over that left parties and trade unions had failed. The most insistent on this were the most ignorant of the history of the left and labour movement. It was as if 8th October 2011 was day zero. One young woman, in response to a lecture on trade unions given by a political and union activist of many years, said that the unions and parties should disband and come here. This was the reality now. They did not have the vocabulary of vanguardism, but they had the mentality on overdrive. On the day of the celebration marking four weeks of the occupation, I updated on Facebook: "After an overdose of people pronouncing on all efforts of the past as having 'failed' and proclaiming a month's encampment as 'the revolution', I'm going to pay my respects to the efforts of the past today, while still trying to play a role in the present. I'll be attending a celebration of the 90th anniversary of the Communist Party of Ireland and then a celebration of 4 weeks of Occupy Dame Street. 90 years. 4 weeks. Let's have some perspective, people."

'Why keep doing the same things that have been tried and failed?' they asked, so knowingly. I reacted to this on many levels. On one level,

I objected to such crude criteria of success and failure. Yes, you could say that the left failed, because we still have capitalism, a capitalism that exploits more effectively than ever, but how much worse would it have been if there had been no resistance, no enunciation of an alternative? I had made the history of the left part of me and I thought of those who lived and died for this movement. I believed that they had brought illumination and solidarity to bear upon the world and I could not write off their lives as failures. Some who said this were so full of themselves in their first flush of activism and so ignorant and arrogant about all that went before them. The lack of historical consciousness was stunning. Do you know, I asked on Facebook, that there was a wave of occupations throughout Ireland many years ago, drawing strength from a powerful global movement. They were called Soviets. So much they did not know. I found their lack of respect for anything that came before them offensive. I kept trying to get across to them that 2011 was not year zero.

At the same time I knew that we could not just go on as before. How many times had we gathered at Parnell Square and marched down O'Connell Street for this and against that and ended up at the GPO or Dáil Éireann or wherever? Were existing socialist or social democratic parties adequate vehicles for the sort of activism appropriate to today? At Occupy Dame Street, I presented myself from day one as old left looking for a new way. I had been a member of the Official Sinn Féin (which became the Workers Party), the Communist Party and the Labour Party. However, even as someone who knew these histories and felt part of these traditions, I found I no longer fit into any of the existing parties of the left. I was between the old and the new. I was not part of any entryist project to recruit new people to these parties, but I tried to persuade them to respect what preceded them and to see themselves within a larger project and a longer story.

At the same time I wanted to see this story move now in a new direction and I saw the Occupy movement as opening a new path. This was a new movement that could not be fit into any of the old moulds, particularly those of vanguardist parties. I was conscious for some time of the existence of an unaffiliated left and felt the need of the sort of movement that would gather these energies into effective analyses and activities. Most of these people came to support the Occupy movement, at least initially, whether to like it on Facebook or to give it their every waking moment. It was a gathering place for these people to find each other, to discuss histories, sensibilities, ideas, plans. Occupy Dame Street opened new spaces, literally as well as metaphorically. It transformed the terrain physically, but also politically. It created a new force on scene. It was not an entirely cohesive force, but it seemed to be a promising one.

The lack of cohesion played itself out particularly in a number of acrimonious assemblies. From the beginning the very mention of trade unions triggered negativity from some elements. Partly this came from a perception that the trade union movement had let the working people down. They had become incorporated in a social partnership process that had left them bereft when shut out of it by government and employers. Trade union officials had lost the skills of class struggle appropriate to the current crisis. Almost everyone coming to ODS agreed with this. However, for some it went beyond this. Speaker after speaker distinguished between the trade union leadership and its members, who needed the trade union movement to serve their needs, but certain elements wanted nothing to do with trade unions. On day three, I delivered and read out to the assembly a statement of support from the Dublin Council of Trade Unions. Those who knew explained to the others that the DCTU had a more radical history than the ICTU (Irish Congress of Trade Unions). Some days later there was another discussion of whether to allow trade unions banners on ODS marches, generating much negativity. The negativity toward trade unions was in almost direct proportion to a lack of experience of them, mainly from students and unemployed youth. Speeches were made for and against trade unions and the proposal failed to achieve consensus.

The next day was our second march. There was great atmosphere at it with singing, dancing, chanting and conversing. RTÉ even put it on the tv news, estimating 2000 on it. Billy Bragg sang when we got to Occupy Dame Street. He bridged the gap between the old and the new powerfully. He sang a few songs about banks and plutocrats, catching the mood of this new movement, and then articulated the need to get support of organised labour and to honour the struggles of the past. He then sang *Power in a Union* and the *Internationale*. It felt great to clench the fist and to sing these songs here and now, ritualising the connection between struggles past and present, between here and everywhere. It was also somewhat healing after the divisive discussion of unions of the night before.

Not long after, the DCTU sent an invitation to ODS to participate in pre-budget march it was planning for 26th November. ODS was also asked to participate in the planning of this march and an ongoing campaign against austerity and to provide a speaker at the march. It was discussed at assembly after assembly. When it finally came to a decision, it was blocked, although the majority of people who are part of ODS in one way or another supported the proposal. This was a veto, dictatorship of minority, many said. Even the most ardent exponents of consensus were among the critics. It was a misuse of the blocking mechanism, they claimed. This has been the most contested decision and it has left bitterness in its wake. A number of people who had been attending assemblies disappeared at this stage.

By this time, there was much evidence of a healthy and progressive relationship between the Occupy movement in the US and organised labour. They sang *Solidarity Forever* and actually enacted many forms of concrete solidarity, from giving material assistance to marching together to blockading ports. Many occupations even had special working groups to reach out to organised labour. Many speakers at ODS assemblies invoked this, but to no avail. The blockers wanted to keep their project pure.

They did not need the left or the unions, they said. They did not seem to need those who came to assemblies or those in working groups either. They had 'the people'. A mystified sense of the people was invoked against anyone who criticised. The people who passed by and said 'good for you' (and maybe did no more) were set against the activists. The people would somehow do what was required (whatever that may be) when the time came. The campers would somehow make it all happen.

The minutes of the general assembly said that, while ODS would not support the march, members of ODS were free to do so. Aside from the ambiguity of what it might mean to be a 'member' of ODS, no one needed ODS to be free to support this march. Some who supported the march, not only attended the march, but set up a group of ODS participants to help organise the march. It was not a democratic centralist organisation after all. Eamonn Crudden, a dynamo of an organiser, pulled together music, posters, leaflets bridging the sensibilities of the Occupy and trade union movements. One demand put forward at an assembly discussing the march was that DCTU stand down their banners when they got to Trinity College out of respect for the area around Dame Street as a banner free zone. This was published in minutes and came in for special scorn on Twitter. Such astonishing arrogance. The other occupations in Ireland, those in Belfast, Galway, Cork, Waterford and Limerick supported the march. After marching, they came to Occupy Dame Street, where there was an assembly of all the occupations. It was an occasion for rallying and singing and celebrating solidarity. I was there, but did not speak on the day. The ODS decision on DCTU was a big breach in the sort of solidarity appropriate to the moment. It was the elephant on the plaza.

Another landmark assembly was one in October that concerned a proposal from the *Enough* campaign to have one joint action with ODS. The SWP came out in numbers that were greater than would be usual at an ODS assembly. This has been the primary evidence cited in charges of SWP attempts to infiltrate ODS. At the assemblies and on the social networks in the days following it there were ugly exchanges, accusations of parasitism and sectarianism, the worst of them coming from the ODS side. I saw it as a positive initiative that would heal the rift created by the rival marches on the international day of solidarity. In terms of process, it was one of the worse I have ever witnessed. The facilitator (in good faith) insisted that, after the proposal was stated, only concerns could be expressed and then amendments to address those concerns. This had the effect of privileging negativity. It meant that for over an hour, only objections to the proposal could be expressed. Some speakers spoke over and over, expressing ugly accusations, before a single positive word was allowed. I objected to this procedure several times before I was permitted to speak in favour. I was one of the few non-members of SWP to do. The proposal was blocked. I stayed around talking to those who had blocked it.

The next day, 29th October, was our third march. The atmosphere at it was terrible. In our pre-march assembly at Parnell Square, a speaker from the *Enough* campaign was booed. At Dame Street, there were further nasty scenes where members of *Enough* / SWP were targeted. This sectarian behaviour, combined with the ignorant and negative attitudes to the trade unions and left parties, made me want to walk away from ODS. Some did walk away. I persisted, but with more difficulty and less enthusiasm. I had a sense of something with great potential unravelling. I tried to carry on and to find a way to harness the positive energies brought into play. At times I was only hanging on by a thread. By 29th October there were approximately 2300 occupations in approximately 2000 cities around the world. I didn't want to leave this movement to those who didn't know what they were doing or did know and were doing it for reactionary reasons.

Oddly enough, there was a *de facto* joint action during the following week. There was a demonstration at the Department of Finance against the payment of an unsecured bond for one billion dollars. Present were ODS along with *Enough* / SWP and *Repudiate the Debt* / CPI. So were the media. I moved between the different groups, all the time worrying that there would be disedifying confrontation. As it turned out, it was an edifying example of left unity. Speakers were evenly divided among the different groups, happening organically using the open mic format. Our numbers were small, but communists, Trotskyists, anarchists and undefined all kept focused on what we were protesting against and who was on the same side in doing so. It was ironic that ODS never had any problem with the *Repudiate the Debt* campaign, which had the same relationship to the CPI that the *Enough* campaign had to the SWP. Yet the fact that the SWP was the force behind the *Enough* campaign was made as an accusation as if it were the worst kind of treachery.

In mid-November, I spoke at the annual Marxism conference organised by the SWP on a panel on the Occupy movement. There were participants in occupations of Belfast, Cork, Galway and Waterford there. They reported no major problems in attitudes to the left and unions. It's not even as if ODS was consistent about acting with other groups or clear about criteria for deciding. There was a ODS contingent with ODS banner on a big student demonstration organised by the Union of Students of Ireland. This was never discussed at a general assembly. It was just done. I was for it, but noted the contradiction. How was acting with USI unproblematic, but DCTU so problematic? As it turned out, the USI stewards and the Gardai blocked the ODS and FEE (Free Education for Everyone) from rejoining the protest after a breakaway action. I was not on that march, deciding to leave that one to another generation.

The generational issue raised itself in my mind as I tried to address my problems in persisting. I noticed that a number of my new left contemporaries in the US were writing about this movement as 'them', analysing what 'they' were doing, thinking, saying. They supported the movement. They visited the occupations. They spoke at the teach-ins.

They marched. But they saw it as essentially the movement of another generation. Perhaps they were right, I thought. Sometimes I felt as if I had wandered into a crèche and I was supposed to pretend to be one of the kids. Perhaps I should see ODS as 'they' and give my judgement on it from a generational distance. Moreover, so many of my contemporaries from my years in the Irish left also seemed to believe that it was time to leave activism to another generation. However, it seemed to me that this was and should be a movement of all ages, even it was the first experience of activism for many of another generation. It made it too easy to dismiss it as a movement of those who were too inexperienced in the ways of the world to know how futile it was.

Even though the new left was more of a youth movement than the Occupy movement is, the old left was still there. I have reminded myself of my new left attitude to the old left. It was sometimes ignorant and arrogant. I later became part of the old left and learned to know and respect what had gone before me. Others had to find their own way. It was perhaps my penance to have inflicted on me some of what I had inflicted on others long ago. Actually some of the younger people, with whom I worked, were impressively mature.

It wasn't only the generational issue that made me wonder about my modus operandi. There was also the perennial tension of the activist intellectual between the time spent on the street and at meetings and the time need to read, think and write about it all. I had often overbalanced towards activism and didn't write what I should have written. I needed to rebalance. After the first month, we expanded the working group for OU and more people became involved in the work. I stopped going to ODS every day, but still went often and remained active in organising and facilitating talks, attending marches and general assemblies. I used the time to try to keep up with the global movement, which had become difficult in the early weeks of intense involvement in the local movement.

At times I had a sense of life cascading so rapidly that it was hard to process it all. One day I wrote that in an e-mail. Within five minutes, I received a call telling me that a colleague had been found dead and a minute later I heard news on radio that Gaddafi had been captured and executed. I did not mourn Gaddafi, but had been following events in Libya with intense interest, since I had been in Tripoli at the outbreak of the uprising. Every day on the news there was so much to take in, from the ongoing hegemony of the markets over states, the crisis of the eurozone, obscene salaries at the top and more cuts to the wages and services of those struggling from below for the basics of life. However, the news of a global movement fighting back was a constant counterweight to all of the terrible news.

How to conceptualise it all? How to assess our impact? I bear the marks of many defeats and could not be so sanguine about what our movement could achieve as many of my younger comrades. Not that we used the term 'comrades' at ODS. It was normally 'peeps'. I look at the world and see so much power and wealth amassed against us. I have seen so many, whom I once considered comrades, so overwhelmed by the realities of this power and wealth that they have more or less changed sides. Currently in Ireland I see those, once in the Workers Party or Labour Left, with whom I once stood, now in government, standing against us, instruments of the global elite, in our lives here. I am standing up against this power and wealth, no longer because I feel confident that we can prevail against it. I keep doing it only so as that they cannot rule uncontested. I do believe that another world is possible, but the odds seem to have mounted as the years have passed.

The young do not tend to see it this way. They are in their first flush of activism and they feel the wind at their backs. They think that somehow they will prevail. They don't quite know how, but they have a sense of their own power and they are high on it. I remember that. I wish that I could still believe in that way, but the years have taught me to assess the balance of forces such as the evidence demands, accustomed as I have become to seeing history unfold disdainful of my desires. I have often invoked Gramsci to myself: pessimism of the intellect, optimism of the will. Optimism of the intellect was much in evidence at ODS. Many of the inspirational quotes posted physically at the site or electronically on Facebook indicated that you could make happen anything you want, if you are determined enough. Not so. A hard lesson learned the hard way.

Actually most of the young people with whom I worked learned a lot in a very short time, in the way that you do in the crucible of practice. They too were critical of the lack of historical consciousness being articulated and were keen to enhance their own knowledge of history, especially the history of the left. Their political judgement was sometimes more astute than some older participants. There were different mentalities that were not reducible to generational patterns.

Both old and young experienced exhilaration, exhaustion, disappointment and revival on the roller coaster ride of the autumn. There was need to take stock as winter came and numbers declined. What did we have to show for it all? Despite all the negativity, something had been achieved. We stood against those who oppress us and we found each other. Many who had been looking around for a way to act, coming along to an occasional protest, but not really fitting into any existing organisations, came together through the Occupy movement and will not retreat. We know each other now. We have shared our stories. We have worked together productively. We have experienced the world in a new way standing together in this new space. Even though we have become alienated from what we have created, we can find another way forward.

The media coverage, although relatively benign, was not in proportion to what the occupation deserved, especially in the early weeks when there was so much activity at ODS. In contrast, the presidential election, which did not deal with any of the real issues facing us, was given saturation coverage. Still RTÉ, TV3 and *Al Jazeera* broadcast from the site, as well as reporting it and having participants on studio panels. Many of the newspaper features went for stories of the occupiers, especially as they found a few who were descendants of occupiers of the GPO in 1916. They homed in on Aubrey Robinson, a serious activist who did not seek the limelight, discovering that he was the son of ex-president Mary Robinson. As a leaderless movement, it discouraged grandstanders. There were a few, especially as numbers thinned, who strutted their stuff for media attention. One was named in two newspapers as 'the leader', although he was far from that, even allowing for the fact that there did emerge informal leadership in this formally leaderless movement.

We did not rely on mainstream media alone. The be-your-own-media approach included website, social networking and video production. Indymedia, Dublin Community TV and Trade Union TV recorded much of the occupation, as did filmmaker Donnacha Ó Briain, whose documentary we have yet to see. There were also blogs, the most consistent being David Johnson's *Booming Back*, giving an upbeat look at ODS without ignoring its more downbeat moments. I did constant diaristic updates on Facebook.

The Garda Síochána adopted a low key presence for most of the life of ODS. They were visibly co-operative, even helpful, at the site and on marches. On one march, I saw a guard miming "We are the 99%", whether consciously or not. What the modus operandi of the special branch was, I did not know, but could guess. The government had not addressed the issue of the occupations or made any move to evict them for four months. The Gardai did indicate that the Central Bank might seek an injunction, especially after more solid wooden structures were erected. On one occasion, ODSers were all day in the courts on standby, listening to cases on fishing and liposuction all day, just in case.

We watched while so many encampments in the US were evicted. I took particular notice of those in Wall Street and Philadelphia. Without any dramatic scenes of police moving in with truncheons and pepper spray, we began to feel a loss of our encampment too. It was less dramatic, but more difficult in its way. The camp versus movement dynamic became increasing unhealthy, playing out in such a way that the movement virtually disappeared, leaving only a camp, more and more preoccupied with its own existence and lashing out at those who disappeared, even though they were the ones who had driven so many people away.

This raised questions of the organisational mode of these occupations, especially this one. The fact that it was open to all meant that it was open to ignorant, addicted, deranged, vainglorious, poisonous people and perhaps agents of hostile forces. Even a few neo-nazis camped for awhile, arguing that they were the 99%. Yet there was increasing hostility to trade unions, to the left, to intellectuals. The negative attitudes and activities of a minority threatened to overwhelm the positive forces set in motion, because the come-all-ye approach, combined with the use of the blocking mechanism and the dominance of the camp over the movement, made it possible for these negative elements to prevail. It was not democracy. It was dictatorship of a minority. It did not prefigure any society we wanted to see.

Numbers turning up for assemblies and marches declined to the point where they became unviable. The march on 10th December gathered only 20 people. I arrived at ODS later, where there was music playing, attracting passing interest, but I recognised few people I knew from assemblies, talks or previous marches.

There were still serious and committed political activists coming and going, even camping, as well as the 'heroes of the revolution' living in their bubble. Both of these were threatened by a criminal element who threatened to shoot or stab the people or burn the place. There were problems with theft, drug dealing and an array of violent behaviour. One admired community activist was thrown out.

Tensions between the media team and the campers reached breaking point and some of the most hard working members of working groups disappeared. We suspended OU talks on 9th December, but met to plan our approach for phase two. Every time I went to ODS in December, there were fewer people there. Even on milder days with many people passing by, there was no one on the street to interact with anyone who wanted to make contact. I went through the barriers on several occasions to find about six people, most of whom I had never seen, who did not seem interested in talking to anyone. I came back on xmas eve with books I had bought for the library wrapped as xmas presents.

There were some good intervals in December. One was the Spectacle of Defiance on 3rd December. Organised for a second year by a coalition of community groups, the ODS assembly made the decision to liaise with it with no concerns, objections or blocks. It was colourful, creative and communal. The theme song of the day was Liam Weldon's *Dark Horse on the Wind* and the words 'Arise. Arise. Arise' echoed through the streets. It started at City Hall with a dark horse ridden by a person in a long flowing black cape and hood, the grim reaper, and ended with a phoenix rising. It stopped at ODS, which joined the march there, just ahead of the phoenix. In early December, there were also protests against the government budget and ODS was on the streets outside Dáil Éireann. There were a number of direct actions in banks and government offices, which were constructive and benignly received by those working in these places.

There was one direct action, though, which was seen as a symptom of degeneration. A group went to Áras an Uachtaráin to invite Michael D. Higgins, the newly-elected president, to come to ODS for a cup of tea. They circulated a 14 minute video on the web, which was painful to watch. It was, according to one ODS supporter on Facebook, familiar with the genre of children's tv, 'a cross between *The Wicker Man* and *Spongebob Squarepants*', and showed ODS disintegrating into political incoherence. There was also a feature on national radio around this time, in which campers indulged in incoherent and deluded talk of revolution. This same commentator, Richard McAleavey, in his blog

Cunning Hired Knaves, put forward a constructive critique of ODS, the most devastating aspect of which was a list of developments occurring in Ireland during the period of the occupation, in relation to the demands, where the situation of the country had deteriorated and we had been further disempowered. ODS had not addressed or acted upon any of these. This was a criticism of us all. A number of people engaged with it in a healthy manner, whereas others responded by pointing out that he wasn't camping, that he was pissing all over their world, that with such friends who needed enemies.

Much of the controversy flared on Facebook for various reasons, including the decline of assemblies. I initiated some of the most acrimonious exchanges, as I believed that some things needed to be said in order to define the situation to decide how to move on from it. I wrote: '"first the problem was the SWP. Then it was DCTU. Or even, more generally, the left and the trade unions. Then it was the media team. Now it is the 'intellectual elite' (defined as people who read books, write blogs, organise talks, articulate criticism). If only it could be just the 'heroes of the revolution' and 'the people' without all these 'parasites' in the way. So where are the people?" This generated many comments.

The new year had got off to a flying start with an occupation of a factory in Cork, a shop in Dublin and a bank in Belfast. An empty office building in Cork was occupied to be transformed into a community resource centre.

The OU working group intended to organise a day of reflection for ODS in the new year. However, too many people, particularly in the working groups, had gone away and didn't want to go on with some of those remaining. Members of the dissident majority gathered in January in Seomra Spraoi, where we discussed bringing the positive energies unleashed by this movement into phase two. It would focus on organising, not camping. It would open out to relations with other groups, such as trade unions. It would initially abandon the open call to all characterising phase one, starting with a circle of people who came to know and trust each other. In response, we were denounced as an elite, as splitters, as parents who threw their children into a fire. Projects such as *Anglo Not Our Debt* and *Unlock NAMA* provided new focus. In January we demonstrated against payment of unsecured bonds in a three day 'carnival of resistance'. We occupied a NAMA building on Great Strand Street to have an economics seminar, although we were evicted by the Gardai in mid-afternoon. There was a new rhythm to it, a slower, steadier rhythm, more aligned to the ordinary rhythm of life.

The truth was that the wave was crashing, here and everywhere. Occupy Cork and Occupy Limerick realised that they were unsustainable and disbanded. There was no such sense of reality in ODS. It was evicted by the Gardai on 8th March, 4 months to the day since it began. By that time, it had degenerated to the point where those many of us who began it were glad to see it end. The evictees continued to do direct actions under the name of ODS, which became more and more ridiculous. When a wealthy couple, landlords with an extensive property portfolio, were evicted from their mansion in Killiney, ODS occupied the sheriff's office and then went to Killiney to demonstrate their solidarity.

OU carried on and ran a 5 Wednesdays in May lecture series on history of radical social movements in Ireland along with Dublin Community TV and the Ireland Institute. In the US many activities continued through the spring of 2012 under the Occupy banner, but the energy had gone out of it.

Globally this was a genuine grassroots manifestation. It unleashed a tide of powerful resistance to global structures of power. It brought new focus, new energy, new fluidity into the convergence of forces confronting a powerful plutocracy. The problems it set out to confront have not been solved. Ireland remains in the firing line of the forces this movement set out to resist. The situation is fluid. 2011 was the year when the voices of the 99% spoke truth to the power of the 1%. We still have not convinced enough of the 99% to resist and the 1% still rule. Nevertheless the class struggle being waged from above has begun to be met with class struggle from below. Another wave will come.

CHAPTER 12
TOWARDS A PUBLIC SPHERE OF EMPOWERMENT AND PARTICIPATION

Mary P. Murphy and Deiric Ó Broin

These chapters have explored recent and historical participative processes from a number of different ideological perspectives and sectoral experiences. A number of conclusions can be identified across the chapters and are discussed here under the broad structure used in the book's framework; partnership, poverty, public policy and public spheres. Three themes, e-participation, power inequalities and protest as participation, surfaced in the various chapters and so are discussed in more detail in this concluding chapter.

Gary Murphy's chapter on partnership reminds us that Ireland did not discover partnership in 1987, rather it had long been open to a corporatist model of key sectors participating in deliberating in economic and social policy. His characterisation of Irish corporatism as 'a dance of strangers' highlights the limitations of Irish corporatism. The partnership approach to public policy which dominated the economy for the last two decades was often portrayed as a problem solving space however it tended to avoid hard choices in favour of easier win-win outcomes and perpetuated an unchallenging group think which proved unsustainable. The real test was not capacity to forge consensus in times of growth but capacity to manage the conflict of crisis and it appears to have at least partially failed this test. The remaining public sector partnership relationship the Croke Park Agreement is due to expire in 2014. It remains to be seen whether partnership has a role in enabling the hard choices that need be made in managing crisis and, as Allen argues, in achieving social justice. Deiric Ó Broin's review of local partnership and participative structures concluded that without the local authority's desire to cede a policy-making role to local citizens and transformative potential of new participative mechanisms on local governance will remain unrealised. All the evidence about the government's agenda for local government reforms points towards a realignment and cohesion of participative structures back into the systems of local government. Without significant local government reform it seems difficult to be optimistic that local partnership is anything but a legimation strategy and service delivery vehicle.

Participation cannot be separated from power and the reality that some people have more power to participate than others. The three chapters on poverty offer very different insights into the experience of participation and deliberation from the perspective of the poor. Matthias Borsheid's chapter in examining the processes through which new ideas and ideological theories permeate our thinking, demonstrates that the issue of structural distribution of resources is not a legitimate concern of ABCD. Ginnell's chapter reflects on the EU as a source of thinking and processes. The well-meaning effort of the European Commission to devise a process of stakeholder consultation was underpinned by a principle that the poor should participate in the process of decision making. However, without the states' willingness or interest in making such policy-making processes work, they can be frustrating experiences that fail to harness their transformative potential. Mike Allen's honest reflection on the experiences of the homeless sector and unemployed people can be used to reflect on wider experiences of poor people and their representative organisations participation in policy processes and wider public debate. Clearly there are limits to the self-organisation of groups where the cause of the immediate poverty (unemployment, homelessness, parenting alone) is not the primary identity of the person. As Allen argues the episodic or transitory nature of unemployment and homelessness has several consequences for attempts to build movements built on identity. This raises the question of how or whether the state should support the role of civil society organisations who mediate between the state and marginalised people. What impact will the state withdrawal of resources have on the inclusion of marginalised people in policy processes?

Elite governance of science is another power structure that requires 'democratic flattening'. There is much cross sectoral learning to be gained from a close reading of the two chapters on public policy which bring us into the brave new world of science policy and the sub-fields of nanotechnology and health diagnostics. Both raise the issue of ethical reasons for enabling public participation, if technology is likely to be all-pervasive, then it needs to be the subject of public discussion. In addition participation has a valuable role to play in shifting public values, public education, creative problem solving and generating new consensus and how society should tackle 'wicked problems'. Further dialogic participation ambitiously anticipates that public engagement might shape discourses and even end products of emerging science. However scientists and policymakers are also motivated to enable public participation to win over public opinion to new technologies and risk scenarios and to mitigate barriers to industrial development and competitiveness. Such dual agendas can make for a sceptical public. For O'Brien the concept of Scientific Citizenship is crucial for enabling both citizen competence in the sciences and active participation in debate. Her focus on the linkages between the public, science and the health diagnostics industry is interesting for the absence of the state as a stakeholder. Murphy's examination of citizens juries as a method of involving the public with nanotechnology is a practical insight into the dogged challenges of involving the public and the time and resources needed. That this pilot tackled issues of marginalisation and challenges of literacy is encouraging. The chapters make clear the link between science and an inclusive society, flattening of power is just as important for participation in the sciences public policy as other areas of policy. State and business resources are required to deepen the relationship between science and society.

All of the chapters have in common a robust belief that the public sphere is important and needs to be meaningfully populated by active citizens. O'Brien for example describes 'dialogue events' that do not seek to influence policy but seek to enable individuals from potentially diverse cultures to come together, articulate positions and views, and interact in a context of genuine equality. Murphy's case study of *Claiming Our Future* and its focus on the core principles of values-led deliberation, cross-sectoral and society-owned spaces is an important insight into how present systems of governance (including political parties) fail to enable mechanisms for legitimate participation. Sheehan's reflections on Occupy's attempt to create a public sphere contrasts with Murphy's. Both chapters reflect that such efforts are not without critique and prove difficult to sustain. Society is demanding not only new forms of governance and public spheres but also a refocus on values and new ideas to create a more sustainable future. There is a lack of dialogue and overlap across the two experiences, an irony given the focus on inter-sectoral alliance building in *Claiming Our Future* and inclusivity in *Occupy*. The two do agree on Drysek's principle (introduced in McInerney's chapter) that civil society requires distance from and autonomy from the state and the importance of society-led creation of public spheres, the two also illustrate the very real challenges of sustaining state-free public spheres.

Inequality

McInerney's opening chapter stressed the importance of power differentials and in particular how participation offers potential to restrict and counter balance the power of business, finance and markets. Gary Murphy's noted the degree to which partnership enabled only limited participation and even then participation was in a context of power hierarchies. Padraig Murphy outlined the need to maximise democratic potential by broadening inclusivity to include diverse publics, including the marginalised voices in society. O'Brien observed the MASIS report's (2011) reflection that participation in public science initiatives in the past decade was concentrated in well-educated, urban, younger sectors of the population.

The three chapters focusing on participation of the poor, homeless and poor communities examined not only the real obstacles to participation but also the limitations to what can be achieved by more micro processes of participation in the absence of broader strategies to tackle and redistribute structural inequalities. None of the chapters in the book offered any gender analysis, nor was there any exploration of the experience of participation by other groups experiencing structural disadvantage and discrimination (including migrants or Travellers, people with disabilities, and the LGBT community). Much of the most severe obstacles to participation are experienced where there is intersectionality of inequality. Sheehan's honest and often poignant reflection gives insight into generational tensions between old and young activist participants.

Taking gender inequality as an example, there is a broader gendered pattern of participation inequality (Murphy 2012). This is not just limiting for women. Patterns of gender inequality in political and public spheres limit our collective capacity and gender equality in public and private decision making is an essential part of a sustainable future. There is a growing awareness about the degree to which gender inequality in governance was a strong contributory factor in causing the initial global and economic crisis. Research confirms women's presence in policy processes alters the process of decision making. While not necessarily less risk adverse, women are more active and independent as board members and directors. This has immediate and strategic application to overall risk management processes, women tend towards more use of committees, weigh long-term priorities and pay more attention to audit and risk oversight and control. TASC concluded that severe gender imbalance and lack of social diversity in participation in corporate governance tends towards 'groupthink' and to decision making that prioritises consensus while ignoring alternative evidence. While women participate more in local community infrastructure they tend not to translate into more formal participative structures like Strategic Policy Committees, this limits participative processes with state/society interfaces. There are significant gender imbalances amongst those representing the interests of businesses and workers in partnership and more informal lobbying processes, this means women's vulnerability in economic downturn is unlikely to receive sufficient focus. The 35% funding cut to the National Women's Council of Ireland in 2012 can only intensify this problem, other national and local women groups are also fire-fight funding cutbacks and coping with pressures on services.

E -participation

Several chapters in this volume noted the use of new technology in enabling participation and observed that the participative web provides both a unique set of opportunities and constraints for deliberation. O'Brien describes the creative methods of the BDI education team sought to adapt and replace the original text-rich format with multimedia elements appropriate for adults with low reading and writing competence and non-native English speakers. *Claiming Our Future* for example made extensive use of the free deliberative software polling, e petitions and web based policy forms as key methods of enabling participation. That Sheehan's article first appeared on blogs is indicative of the power of such new forums and their use in the *Occupy* movement, she however discounts the idea of Facebook or Twitter revolutions arguing the impetus really comes from real social conditions and relations, while technologies greatly enhance the capacity to connect and to build social movements. The internet is said to have transformed three factors fundamental for policy-making: knowledge, connections and individuals embedded in networks (Liston *et al.* 2012). Online forums provide a unique opportunity for integrating citizen deliberation to the policy process on an on-going basis. Examples of online deliberation are emerging and include participatory budgeting, city planning, deliberative opinion polls, online political discussion networks and online town hall meetings. Yet to date public authorities have, for the most part, used the internet for service delivery and information provision and dissemination. To this extent we have had more e-government than e-democracy. Komito's review of e-governance, new technologies, local government and civic participation shows a clear evidence of interest in policy participation but inadequate structures to facilitate participation (2012: 197). In common with the OECD 2003 review he finds little mainstreaming and 'little evidence of new technologies that encourage significant numbers of citizens to participate in policy formation'. Komito offers, as an example, *Mobhaile,* a pilot project established in 2004 to progress e-government and e-participation functions. While this had technological potential its capacity was reliant on the local authority's desire to cede a policy making role to local citizens and Komito found no evidence they wanted to do this electroncially or otherwise. Consistent with many contributors to this volume (Ó Broin, Borsheid and Ginnell) he concludes that without desire the transformative potential of new technologies on governance will remain unrealised.

That is not to say there is no impact from new technology, Komito (2012) observes that Irish politics has shifted from mediation with individuals in a clientalistic and brokerage culture to mediation with interest groups and that a specific contribution has been the way new technologies have enhanced general and specific access to information. On the other hand the ease to which individuals can use new technologies (to blog, set up Facebook campaigns etc) might lead to a pattern of individual rather than collective action (Kirby and Murphy 2011; Ó Broin and Moore 2011). Assuming that internet-based media may overcome the limitations of traditional media may be over-optimistic. E-Participation is also heavily gendered and there is a significant age and socioeconomic digital divide, new media can mirror and perpetuate existing unequal patterns of participation (Bua 2009).

Protest

A previous publication in this series *Power Dissent and Politics, Civil Society and the State in Ireland* interrogated the relationship between state and society in Ireland (Ó Broin and Kirby 2009). It concluded there was to some degree an absence of a culture of conflict and ideological debate in Ireland. Carney and Harris (2012) argue Irish civil society organisations are adjusting to the impact of the economic crisis and the partial collapse of Irish social partnership corporatist structures by adapting lobbying techniques to include street protests, media campaigns, and social media communication strategies. It is still too soon to see what impact the replacement of social partnership by 'social dialogue' will have on the dynamics of participation in decision-making in Ireland. As chapters by Mary P. Murphy and Helena Sheehan show, the lack of trust in the political sphere and political institutions is translating into some (but not significant) demand from citizens in the form of protest and calls for greater participation. It is notable that these take the form of peaceful deliberative processes rather than more dissent oriented street protest. Padraig Murphy also notes in the area of nanotechnology real tensions and conflict in local public arenas where there are socio-technical disputes. Real fears of (and experience of) corporatist bullying are a significant obstacle to participation.

Lowenstein *et al.* (2007) define protest as a traditional and essential form of participation in policy making in a democracy, protest and dissent about the status quo is a public expression of policy preferences demands and of stating citizens' and migrants' frustrations with state policies. Since the current economic crisis took hold international commentators congratulated Irish society on its mature response to budget cuts and many mainstream commentators perceive a passivity in Irish society response to the crisis. The late Peter Mair (2010: 7) describes a 'passive' and 'demobilised' citizenry. However, since 2008 pensioners, students, workers, parents and disadvantaged communities have mounted various responses to austerity and cutbacks and used demonstrations, petitions, meetings, marches and creative 'spectacles of defiance' to register protest against health and education closures and social welfare cuts. These have been local as well as national. Sheehan records a significant level of protest activity in the Occupy movement and related campaigns. Issues pertaining to local environmental issues have significant capacity to animate local protest. Padraig Murphy describes the socio-technical nature of science and sub politics which intensifies when fuelled by economic and political disillusionment. The Rossport protest predated the crisis and anti-fracking campaigns have potential to be a major source of tension between state and society.

The most vociferous protest, the household charge campaign, while clearly challenging the state, has to date been a largely peaceful protest. It is not clear whether this pattern of relatively peaceful protest will prevail or whether as unemployment stays stubbornly high (14.9% in July 2012) the nature of state-society relations will shift to a more conflictual pattern of contestation. Allen's chapter, however, gives some insight that high unemployment or social trauma does not necessarily translate into protest. He does however raise the interesting question as to how we understand the function and power of protest and how this relates to the function and power of disruption and argues for a wider yet more strategic concept of what can be done by the poor to disrupt public policy making.

Conclusion

Kirby and Murphy (2009) argue that fundamental transformative change will not come about without participation in open communicative discourse about values. Habermas (2006: 103) speaks of the importance of a political public sphere, significant policy change requires public communication and discourse. This means a pivotal focus on the role of the media. Many are rightly critical of the role of the Irish media in framing politics, policy and power. Participation in public debate and an inclusive mainstream media community is crucial for healthy democracy. The Carnegie Trust (2007) points to issues of ownership of new and old forms of media. Sheehan points to the important lesson from *Occupy*, what she calls the be-your-own-media approach. It is ironic that government's support for the community infrastructure (once highlighted as an example of good practice to other Member States) is now being dismantled with severe consequences for participation. Padraig Murphy notes the dialogical models of the future require significant commitments from what he describes as already over-stretched community workers.

Stoker (2012) identifies public participation and deliberation as necessary ingredients to deliver a politics that is capable of addressing crisis, managing loss and building coalitions of long-term policy support for more sustainable alternative economic strategies. He notes this needs to involve bypassing electoral constraints by developing a more deliberative dialogue with citizens and a different form of institutionalised power sharing giving a much wider role to interests and local and regional government. There is increasing demand for creative public space for political and policy debate and there is a particular challenge of including people experiencing poverty in new public spheres. While this space needs to be some distance from and autonomous of the state there is also an obligation on the state and society, in facilitating a functioning and effective democracy, to make sure public spheres are challenging, participative and inclusive of all. However this should not over stress what can be achieved through such participation. As Allen argues, given the difficulty of meaningful mobilisation of people experiencing socio-economic rather than identity-based marginalisation (although these are clearly linked), solidarity is at least as important as inclusive participation. As McInerney argues there is a weak relationship between meaningful public participation and the institutions of representative democracy at both local and national level. We should be mindful that there is a very distinct and growing distance between the aspiration for greater public participation in public policy making and the reality of how policy is actually determined.

References

A

Acheson, Nicholas, Brian Harvey and Arthur Williamson. 2004. *Two Paths, One Purpose: Voluntary Action in Ireland North and South*. Dublin: Institute of Public Administration.

Advocacy Initiative. 2010. *Advocacy Initiative Project Report*. Dublin: Advocacy Initiative.

Allen, Mike. 2006. *The Bitter Word: Ireland's Jobs Famine and its Aftermath*. Dublin: Poolbeg.

Allen, Mike. 2009. 'The Political Organisation of People Who Are Homeless: Reflections of a Sympathetic Sceptic', in *European Journal of Homelessness*, Volume 3: 289-299.

Amin, Ash and Nigel Thrift. 1995. 'Institutional issues for the European regions: from markets and plans to socioeconomics and powers of association', in *Economy and Society*, Volume 24 (1): 41- 66.

Anderson, Alison, Alan Petersen, Clare Wilkinson and Stuart Allan. 2009. *Nanotechnology, Risk and Communication*. London: Palgrave Macmillan.

Anker, Jørgen. 2008. 'Organizing homeless people: Exploring the emergence of a user organization in Denmark', in *Critical Social Policy*, Volume 28(1): 27-50.

B

Bainbridge, William Sims 2002. 'Public attitudes toward nanotechnology', in *Journal of Nanoparticle Research* Volume 4 (6): 561–570.

Baker John, Kathleen Lynch, Sara Cantillon and Judy Walsh. 2004. *Equality: From Theory to Action*. Basingstoke: Palgrave Macmillan.

Barber, Benjamin. 1984. *Strong Democracy: Participatory Politics for a New Age*. Berkeley: University of California Press.

Barnes, Marian, Janet Newman and Helen Sullivan. 2007. *Power, Participation and Political Renewal: Case studies in public participation*. Bristol : Policy Press.

Beck, Ulrich. 1992. *Risk Society: Towards a New Modernity*. London: Sage.

Breeze, Jonathan Turner Ruth, and Patterson Paul 2003. *Anti-Community Behaviour: Ballymun Citizens' Jury Report*. Dublin: Vision 21.

Broderick, Sheelagh. 2002. 'Community Development in Ireland: a policy review', in *Community Development Journal*, Volume 37 (1): 101-110.

Bua, Adrian. 2009. 'Realising Online Democracy: A Critical Appraisal of Online Civic Commons', in Think Piece 51, available at http://clients.squareeye.net/uploads/compass/documents/CTP51BauDemocracy last accessed 18th November 2012.

Bucchi, Massimiano. 2004. *Science in Society: An Introduction to Social Studies of Science*. Oxford: Routledge.

Buechler, Stephen M. 1995. 'New Social Movement Theories', in *Sociological Quarterly*, Volume 36 (3): 441-464.

Burawoy, Michael. 2003. 'For a Sociological Marxism: The Complementary Convergence of Antonio Gramsci and Karl Polanyi', in *Politics & Society*, Volume 31 (2): 193-261.

Burton, Paul. 2007. 'Conceptual, theoretical and practical aspects in measuring the impact of citizen participation in policy making', Paper to CINEFOGO Conference in Bristol, England 14-15 February 2007 available at http://cinefogoconference.pbworks.com/f/PN024_Burton.pdf last accessed 18th November 2012.

C

Callon, Michel. 1986. 'Some Elements of a Sociology of Translation: Domestication of the Scallops and the Fishermen of St. Brieuc Bay', in John Law (ed.) *Power, Action and Belief: A New Sociology of Knowledge?* London: Routledge and Kegan Paul.

Carnegie Trust, 2007. *Inquiry into the future of civil society in the UK and Ireland.* London: Carnegie UK Trust.

Carney, Gemma and Clodagh Harris. 2012. *Citizens' Voices: Experiments in Democratic Renewal and Reform.* Galway: IRCHSS, PSAI and Irish Centre of Social Gerontology.

Castells, Manuel. 2009. *Communication Power.* Oxford: Oxford University Press.

Changing Ireland. 2010. 'Claiming Our Future: People Power Must Prevail', in *Changing Ireland*, Number 34. Limerick: Changing Ireland.

Christian, Julie, Christopher J. Armitage and Dominic Abrams. 2003. 'Predicting uptake of housing services: The role of self-categorization in the theory of planned behaviour', in *Current Psychology*, Volume 22 (3): 206-217.

Cicero. [51BC] 2009. *On the Republic.* Oxford: Oxford University Press.

Combat Poverty Agency. 2000. *Guidelines for Effective Involvement* – Published as part of project co-funded by the European Commission under the Programme for Preparatory Actions to Combat and prevent Social Exclusion. Dublin: Combat Poverty Agency.

Combat Poverty Agency. 2006. *Better Policies, Better Outcomes – Promoting Mainstreaming Social Inclusion.* Dublin: Combat Poverty Agency.

Combat Poverty Agency. 2009. *People, Poverty and Participation.* Dublin: Combat Poverty Agency.

Communities First Task Force. 2007. *Bowling Together in the City - An Action Plan for Social Capital and Active Citizenship in Dublin City.* Dublin: Dublin City Council.

Connolly, Eileen. 2007. *The Institutionalisation of Anti Poverty and Social Exclusion Policy in Irish Social Partnership.* Dublin: Dublin City University/Combat Poverty Agency.

Cornwall, Andrea. 2002. *Making spaces, changing places: situating participation in development.* Working Paper 170. Sussex: Institute of Development Studies.

Cornwall, Andrea. 2004 'New Democratic Spaces: The Politics of Institutionalised Participation', in *Institute of Development Studies Bulletin*, Volume 35 (2): 1-10.

Cox, Lawrence. 2010. 'Another World is Under Construction. Social Movement Responses to Inequality and Crisis' paper to *Equality in a time of crisis*. Egalitarian World Initiative/ UCD School of Social Justice, UCD, May 7th 2010.

Cox, Lawrence. 2012. 'Challenging Austerity in Ireland: Community and Movement Responses' in Concept, Vol.3 (2): 1-6

Cress, Daniel M. and David A. Snow. 1996. 'Mobilization at the Margins: Resources, Benefactors, and the Viability of Homeless Social Movement Organizations' in *American Sociological Review*, Volume 61 (6): 1089-1109.

Cronin, Michael. 2009. 'Active Citizenship and its Discontents', in Deiric Ó Broin and Peadar Kirby (eds) *Power, Dissent and Democracy: Civil Society and the state in Ireland*. Dublin: A&A Farmar.

Crowley, Una and Rob Kitchin. 2007. 'Paradoxical spaces of Traveller citizenship in contemporary Ireland', in *Irish Geography*, Volume 40 (2): 128-145.

Culhane, Dennis P. and Stephen Metraux. 2008. 'Rearranging the Deck Chairs or Reallocating the Lifeboats? Homelessness Assistance and Its Alternatives', in *Journal of the American Planning Association*, Volume 74 (1): 111- 121.

D

Davies, Keith G. and Wolf-Philips, Jonathan. 2006. 'Scientific Citizenship and good governance: implications for biotechnology', in *TRENDS in Biotechnology*, Volume 24 (2): 57-61.

Davies, Sarah, Ellen McCallie, Elin Simonsson, Jane L. Lehr and Sally Duensing. 2009. 'Discussing dialogue: perspectives on the value of science dialogue events that do not inform policy', in *Public Understanding of Science*, Volume 18 (3): 338-353.

Delgado, Ana, Kamilla Lein Kjølberg and Fern Wickson. 2011. 'Public engagement coming of age: From theory to practice in STS encounters with nanotechnology', in *Public Understanding of Science*, Volume 20 (6): 826-845.

Donaldson, Ken, Vicki Stone, Lang Tran, Wolfgang Kreyling and Paul Borm. 2004. 'Nanotoxicology', in *Occupational and Environmental Medicine*, Volume 61 (9): 727-728.

Drexler, K. Eric. 1986. *Engines of Creation: The Coming Era of Nanotechnology*. New York: Anchor Books/Doubleday.

Dryzek, John. 1996. 'Political inclusion and the dynamics of democratization, in *American Political Science Review*, Volume 90 (3): 475-487.

Dryzek, John. 2000. *Deliberative Democracy and Beyond: Liberals, Critics, Contestations*. Oxford: Oxford University Press.

Dryzek, John 2007. 'Theory, Evidence and the Tasks of Deliberation', in Shawn W. Rosenberg (ed.) *Deliberation, Participation and Democracy, Can the People Govern?*, Basingstoke: Palgrave MacMillan.

Dublin City Council. 2008. *Community and Neighbourhood Development Strategy 2008-2012*. Dublin: Dublin City Council.

E

EAPN. 2003. *Where is the Political Energy? – EAPN's Response to the Second Round of Plans*. Brussels: EAPN.

EAPN Ireland. 2008. *Shadow Report on Ireland's NAP Inclusion 2008-2010*. Dublin: EAPN Ireland.

EAPN. 2009. *Small Steps- big changes: Building Participation of People Experiencing Poverty*. Brussels: EAPN.

EAPN Ireland and the Community Platform. 2003. *Response to the NAP Inclusion 2003-2005*. Community Platform.

EAPN Ireland and the Community Platform. 2005. *Response to the Second Irish National Action Plan Against Poverty and Social Exclusion 2003-2005*. Community Platform.

Edwards, Michael. 2005. 'Civil society', in *The Encyclopedia of Informal Education*, available at www.infed.org/ association/civil_society.htm last accessed 17th November 2012.

Etzkowitz, Henry. 2008. *The Triple Helix – University-Industry-Government Innovation in Action*. New York and London – Routledge

European Commission. 2001. *European Governance – A White Paper*. Brussels: European Commission.

European Commission. 2002. *Joint Report on Social Exclusion*. Brussels: European Commission.

European Commission. 2003. *Joint Report on Social Exclusion*. Brussels: European Commission.

European Commission. 2004. *Communication from the Commission: Towards a European Strategy for Nanotechnology*. Brussels: European Commission.

European Commission. 2006a. *Common Objectives on Social Protection and Social Inclusion*. Brussels: European Commission.

European Commission. 2006b. *Joint Reports on Social Protection and Social Inclusion*. Brussels: European Commission.

European Commission. 2006c. *Europeans and Biotechnology in 2005: Patterns and Trends - Eurobarometer 55.2*. Brussels: European Commission.

European Commission. 2007a. *Joint Report on Social Protection and Social Inclusion*. Brussels: European Commission.

European Commission. 2007b. *Joint Report on Social Protection and Social Inclusion- Supporting Document SEC (2007) 329*. Brussels: European Commission.

European Commission. 2007c. *Joint Report on Social Protection and Social Inclusion- Country Report SEC (2007) 272*. Brussels: European Commission.

European Commission. 2008. *Guidance Note for Preparing National Strategy Reports for Social Protection and Social Inclusion 2008-2010*. Brussels: European Commission.

European Commission. 2009. *Joint Report on Social Protection and Social Inclusion*. Brussels: European Commission.

European Commission. 2010a. *The Social Situation in the European Union 2009*, Brussels.

European Commission. 2010b. Europe 2020: *A Strategy for Smart, Sustainable and Inclusive Growth*. Brussels.

European Commission. 2010c. *Science and Technology* Special Eurobarometer 73.1. Brussels: European Commission

European Council. 2000. 'Presidency Conclusions', Lisbon European Council of 23th and 24th March 2000, available at http://www.europarl.europa.eu /summits/lis1_en.htm last accessed November 17th 2012.

European Union. 2007. *Treaty of Lisbon*. Official Journal of the European Union. Brussels.

F

Felt, Ulrike, Brian Wynne, Michel Callon, Maria Eduarda Gonçalves, Sheila Jasanoff, Maria Jepsen, Pierre-Benoît Joly, Zdenek Konopasek, Stefan May, Claudia Neubauer, Arie Rip, Karen Siune, Andy Stirling, A. Mariachiara Tallacchini. 2007. *Taking European Knowledge Society Seriously - Report of the Expert Group on Science and Governance, to the Science, Economy and Society Directorate, Directorate-General for Research, European Commission*. Brussels, Belgium: European Commission

Feynman, Richard. 1959. 'There's Plenty of Room at the Bottom', available at http://www.zyvex.com/nanotech/feynman.html, last accessed 17th November 2012.

Fitzgibbon, Gearóid. 2010. 'Is Féidir Linn: A new departure or a wish list for Santa', in *Changing Ireland*, Number 33. Limerick: Changing Ireland.

Forfás. 2010. Ireland's Nanotechnology Commercialisation Framework 2010-2014. Dublin: Government Publications.

Forfás: 2011a. Research and Development Funding and Performance in the State Sector 2009 – 2010 Dublin: Government Publications.

Forfás: 2011b. *Strategy for Science, Technology and Innovation Indicators 2011*. Dublin: Government Publications.

Forfás. 2012. Report of the Research Prioritisation Group. Dublin: Government Publications.

Friends of the Earth. 2010. *Nanotechnology, climate and energy: over-heated promises and hot air*? Melbourne: Friends of the Earth

Fung, Archon and Eric Olin Wright. 2001. 'Deepening Democracy: Innovations in Empowered Participatory Governance', in *Politics and Society*, Volume 29 (1): 5-41.

Fung, Archon and Eric Olin Wright. 2003. *Deepening Democracy: Institutional Innovations in Empowered Participatory Governance*. London: Verso.

Fuller, Steve. 2011. *Humanity 2.0: What it Means to Human Past, Present and Future*. Basingstoke: Palgrave Macmillan.

G

Gaskell, George, Nick Allum, Martin Bauer, Jonathan Jackson, Susan Howard and Nicola Lindsey. 2003. *Ambivalent GM nation? Public attitudes to biotechnology in the UK, 1991–2002*. London: London School of Economics.

Gavelin, Karen, Richard Wilson and Robert Doubleday. 2007. *Democratic Technologies? The final report of the Nanotechnology Engagement Group*. Involve: London.

Gaynor, Niamh. 2009. 'In-Active Citizenship and the depoliticisation of community development in Ireland', in *Community Development Journal*, Volume 46 (1): 9-36.

Geoghegan, Martin and Fred Powell. 2009. 'Community development, the Irish state and the contested meaning of civil society', in Deiric Ó Broin and Peadar Kirby (eds) *Power, Dissent and Democracy: Civil Society and the Irish State*. Dublin: A&A Farmer.

Giddens, Anthony. 1991. *Modernity and Self-identity: Self and Society in the Late Modern Age*. Cambridge, UK: Polity Press

Government of Ireland. 2000b. *A White Paper on a Framework for Supporting Voluntary Activity and for Developing the Relationship between the State and the Community and Voluntary Sector*. Dublin: Stationery Office.

Government of Ireland. 2006. *Strategy for Science, Technology and Innovation 2006-2013*. Dublin: Government Publications.

Government of Ireland. 2008. *Building Ireland's Smart Economy - A Framework for Sustainable Economic Renewal*. Dublin: Government Publications.

Government of Ireland. 2010. *The Report of the Innovation Taskforce*. Dublin: Government Publications.

Green, Mike, Henry Moore and John O'Brien. 2006. *ABCD in Action: When People Care Enough to Act*. Toronto: Inclusion Press.

Gregory, Jane and Steven Miller. 1998. *Science in Public: Communication, Culture and Credibility*. New York: Plenum

Guston, David and Daniel Sarewitz. 2002. 'Real-time technology assessment', in *Technology in Society*, Volume 24 (1): 93–109.

H

Habermas, Jürgen. 2006. 'The Public Sphere', in Robert E. Goodin and Philip Pettit (eds) *Contemporary Political Philosophy: An Anthology*. Oxford: Blackwell Publishing.

Hardiman, Niamh, 1988. *Pay, Politics and Economic Performance in Ireland 1970–1987*. Oxford: Clarendon Press.

Harvey, Brian. 2004. *Implementing the White Paper Supporting Voluntary Activity: Report for the CV12 Group*. Dublin: The Wheel.

Harvey, Brian. 2009a. *No Strings Attached*. Dublin: Community Platform.

Harvey, Brian. 2009b. 'Ireland and civil society: reaching the limits of dissent', in Deiric Ó Broin and Peadar Kirby (eds) *Power, Dissent and Democracy, Civil Society and the Irish State*. Dublin: A&A Farmer.

Harvey, David. 2005. *A Brief History of Neoliberalism*. Oxford: Oxford University Press.

Hastings Tim, Brian Sheehan and Padraig Yeates. 2007. *Saving the Future: How Social Partnership shaped Ireland's Economic Success*. Dublin: Blackhall.

Hay, Colin. 2004. 'Ideas, Interests and Institutions in the Comparative Economy of Great Transformations', in *Review of International Political Economy*, Volume 2 (1): 204-226.

Hay, Colin, Michael Lister and David Marsh. 2006. *The State: Theories and Issues*. Basingstoke: Palgrave Macmillan

Hayles, Katherine. 2004. 'Connecting the Quantum Dots: Nanotechnoscience and Culture', in Katherine Hayles (ed) *Nanoculture: Implications of the New Technoscience*. Bristol: Intellect Books.

Healey, Patsy. 2006. *Collaborative Planning: Shaping Places in Fragmented Societies*. Basingstoke: Palgrave Macmillan.

Held, David. 1989. *Political Theory and the Modern State*. Cambridge: Polity Press.

Hilgartner, Stephen. 1990. 'The Dominant View of Popularization: Conceptual Problems, Political Uses', in *Social Studies of Science*, Volume 20 (3): 519-539.

Horgan, John, 1997. *Seán Lemass: The Enigmatic Patriot*. Dublin: Gill and Macmillan.

Horst, Maja. 2007. 'Public Expectations of Gene Therapy: Scientific Futures and their Performative Effects on Scientific Citizenship', in *Science, Technology and Human Values*, Volume 32 (2): 150-171.

Hough, Jennifer. 2012. 'Advisers back all-Ireland anti-fracking campaign', in The Irish Examiner February 17th 2012, available at: http://www.irishexaminer.com/ireland/advisers-back-all-ireland-anti-fracking-campaign-184164.html, last accessed November 17th 2012.

Hullman, Angela. 2006. *The Economic Development of Nanotechnology – An Indicators Based Analysis*. Brussels: European Commission.

I

ICSTI. 1999. *Technology Foresight Ireland- An ICSTI Overview*. Dublin: Forfás.

Irwin, A. 2001. Constructing the Scientific Citizen: Science and Democracy in the Biosciences', in *Public Understanding of Science*, Volume 10 (1): 1-18.

Is Feidir Linn. 2009. *Shaping our Future*, Dublin: Is Feidir Linn.

K

Kirby, Peadar. and Mary P. Murphy. 2009. 'State and civil society in Ireland: conclusions and mapping alternatives', in Deiric Ó Broin and Peadar Kirby (eds) *Power, Dissent and Democracy: Civil Society and the Irish State*. Dublin: A&A Farmer.

Kirby Peadar and Mary .P. Murphy. 2011. *Towards a Second Republic: Irish Politics after the Celtic Tiger*. London: Pluto.

Kolsto, Stein Dankert. 2001. 'Scientific Literacy for Citizenship: Tools for Dealing with the Science Dimension of Controversial Socioscientific Issues', in *Science Education*, Volume 85 (3): 291-310.

Komito, Lee. 2012 'E-governance new technologies, local government and civic engagement', in Niamh Hardiman (ed) *Irish Governance in Crisis*. Manchester: Manchester University Press.

Kretzman, John and John McKnight. 1993. *Building Communities from the Inside Out: A Path Toward Finding and Mobilizing a Community's Assets*. Chicago: Northwestern University Press.

KurzweilAI.net. 2012. (Homepage). [Online]. Available at http://www.kurz weilai.net, last accessed November 17th 2012.

L

Larragy, Joe. 2004. 'Irish social partnership: what is the significance of the community-voluntary pillar', paper presented at *IN: Conference and Workshop 'Social Partnership: A New Kind of Governance'* 14–15 September 2004 at NUI Maynooth, available at *http://sociology. nuim. ie/conferencessocialpartnerships. Html* last accessed November 17th 2012.

Lash, Scott. 1994. 'Reflexivity and its doubles', in Ulrich Beck, Anthony Giddens, and Scott Lash (eds) *Reflexive Modernisation: Politics, Tradition, and Aesthetics in the Modern Social Order*. Cambridge: Polity Press.

Latour, Bruno. 2004. *The Politics of Nature: How to Bring the Sciences into Democracy*. Cambridge: Cambridge University Press.

Lee, Joe. 1989. *Ireland 1912-1985: Politics and Society*. Cambridge: Cambridge University Press.

Linders, Annulla and Marina Kalander. 2007. 'The Construction and Mobilization of Unemployed Interests: The Case of Sweden in the 1990s', in *Qualitative Sociology*, Volume 30(4): 417-437.

Lippmann, Walter. 1993 [1927]. *The Phantom Public*. New Brunswick: Transaction Publishers.

Liston, Vanessa, Mark O'Toole, Clodagh Harris and Khurshid Ahmad. 2012. 'A Theoretical Framework for Enabling Computer Mediated Deliberative Democracy', available at http://wwwacademia.edu/575718/A_Theoretical_ Framework_for_Enabling_Computer_Mediated_Deliberative_Democracy_in_Ir eland, last accessed November 18th 2012.

Lowenstein Frank, Sheryl Lechner and Erik Brunn. 2007. *Voices of Protest!: Documents of Courage and Dissent*. New York: Black Dog and Leventhal.

M

MacConnell, Seán. 2007a. "Minister accused of trying to close local development company" in *The Irish Times*, 27th August 2007.

MacConnell, Seán. 2007b. "Challenge to rules of EU rural scheme" in *The Irish Times*, 19th October 2007.

MacConnell, Seán. 2008a. "Co-op takes LEADER revamp case to European Commission" in *The Irish Times*, 7th March 2008.

MacConnell, Seán. 2008b. "Rural groups urged to elect boards" in *The Irish Times*, 13th June 2008.

MacConnell, Seán. 2008c. "Minister hints at time extension for development plans" in *The Irish Times*, 20th June 2008.

MacConnell, Seán. 2008d. "Hold elections or lose funds, Ó Cuiv warns LEADER groups" in *The Irish Times*, 23rd June 2008.

McCann, Dermot, 1993. 'Business power and collective action: the state and the Confederation of Irish Industry 1970–1990', in *Irish Political Studies*, Volume 8 (1): 37–53.

McCarthy, John D. and Mayer N. Zald. 1977. 'Resource Mobilization and Social Movements: A Partial Theory', in *American Journal of Sociology*, Volume 83 (6): 1212-1241.

McGuirk, Pauline. 2003. 'The future of the city: a geography of connection and disconnection', in *Geodate*, Volume 16 (4): 5-8.

McInerney, Chris. 2011. *Building Effective Consultation and Participation: Lessons Learned from outside Ireland*. Dublin: EAPN Ireland.

Mair, Peter. 2010 'Paradoxes and Problems of Modern Irish Politics', paper presented to the *McGill Summer School: Reforming the Republic* July 2010.

Manor, James, Mark Robinson and Gordon White. 1999. *Civil Society and Governance - A Concept Paper*, Institute of Development Studies, available at http://cide.oise.utoronto.ca/civil_society/resources/Manor%20Robinson%20and %20White%20Concept%20Paper.pdf , last accessed November 18th 2012.

MASIS. 2011. *Monitoring Policy and Research Activities on Science in Society in Europe (MASIS) - National Report Ireland*, available at http://www.masis.eu/english/storage/publications/nationalreports/masisnation alreportireland, last accessed November 18th 2012.

Masters, Adam. 2009. 'Republic of Ireland: from Celtic tiger to recession victim', in Paul 't Hart and Karen Tindall (eds), *Framing the Global Economic Downturn: Crisis Rhetoric and the Politics of Recession*. Canberra: ANU Press.

Mejlgaard, Niels and Sally Stares. 2010. 'Participation and competence as joint components in a cross-national analysis of scientific citizenship', in *Public Understanding of Science*, Volume 19 (5): 545-561.

Milburn, Colin. 2004. 'Nanotechnology in the Age of Posthuman Engineering: Science Fiction as Science', in Katherine Hayles (ed) *Nanoculture: Implications of the New Technoscience*. Bristol: Intellect Books.

Murphy, Gary. 2003. 'Towards a corporate state? Seán Lemass and the realignment of interest groups in the policy process 1948–1964', in *Administration*, Volume 51 (1–2): 105–18.

Murphy, Gary. 2009. *In search of the promised land: the politics of post war Ireland.* Cork: Mercier Press.

Murphy, Gary and John Hogan, 2008. 'Fianna Fáil, the Trade Union Movement and the Politics of Macroeconomic Crises, 1970-82', in *Irish Political Studies,* Volume 23 (4): 577-98.

Murphy, Gary and Conor McGrath. 2011. 'The Curious Case of Lobbying in Ireland: An Introduction', in *Journal of Public Affairs*, Volume 11 (2): 71-73.

Murphy, Mary P. and Peadar Kirby. 2008. *A Better Ireland is Possible - towards an alternative vision for Ireland.* Dublin: Community Platform.

Murphy Mary P. 2012. 'Irish Civil Society in the Shadow of the Irish State', in *Irish Journal of Sociology,* Volume 19 (2): 173-189.

Murphy, Padraig. 2009. 'The challenges of "upstream" communication and public engagement for Irish nanotechnology', in Simone Arnaldi, Andrea Lorenzet and Federico Russo (eds) *Technoscience in Progress: Managing the Uncertainty of Nanotechnology.* Amsterdam: IOS Press.

Murphy, Padraig. 2010. *Nanotechnology: Public Engagement with Health, Environmental and Social Issues.* Dublin: Environmental Protection Agency.

Murray, Catherine and Paul Rogers. 2009. 'Community development: a practitioners' perspective', in Deiric Ó Broin and Peadar Kirby (eds) *Power, Dissent and Democracy: Civil Society and the Irish State.* Dublin: A&A Farmer.

N

Nanojury. 2005. (Homepage). [Online]. Available from: http://www.nano-jury.org.uk/index.html [Accessed 23 February 2010].

National Economic and Social Council. 1986. *Strategy For Development.* Dublin: NESC.

National, Economic and Social Forum. 2003. *Inaugural Meeting of the NAPS Social Inclusion Forum –Conference Report.* Dublin: NESF.

National, Economic and Social Forum. 2007. Conference Report - Fourth Meeting of the Social Inclusion Forum. Dublin: NESF.

National, Economic and Social Forum. 2008. *Conference Report - Fifth Meeting of the Social Inclusion Forum.* Dublin: NESF.

National Science Foundation. 2012. *Budget FY 2012,* available at http://www.genome.gov/Pages/About/Budget/NHGRIFY2012CJ.pdf, last accessed November 18th 2012.

Narayan, D., Chambers, R., Shah, M. K. and Petesch, P. (2000) *Voices of the Poor: Crying Out for Change,* New York: Oxford University Press for the World Bank.

Nowotny, Helga, Peter Scott and Michael Gibbons. 2001. *Re-thinking Science: Knowledge and the Public in an Age of Uncertainty.* Cambridge: Polity Press.

O

OECD. 2001. *Citizens as Partners – OECD Handbook on Information, Consultation and Public Participation in Policy-Making.* Paris: OECD.

OECD. 2003. *Promise and Problems of E-Democracy – Challenges of Online Citizen Engagement.* Paris: OECD.

OECD. 2008. Directorate for Science, Technology and Industry Committee for Science and Technological Policy Conference on Outreach and Public Engagement in Nanotechnology in Delft, Netherlands, October 30th 2008, available at: http://www.oecd.org/document/17/0,3746,en_21571361_41212117_42324625_1_1_1_1,00.html, last accessed November 18th 2012.

Ó Broin, Deiric. 2009. 'Institutionalising social partnership in Ireland', in Deiric Ó Broin and Peadar Kirby (eds) *Power, Dissent and Democracy: Civil Society and the State in Ireland.* Dublin: A&A Farmar.

Ó Broin, Deiric and Peadar Kirby. 2009. 'Creating a parallel state: the development of community-based movements in the late 19th and early 20th centuries', in Deiric Ó Broin and Peadar Kirby (eds) *Power, Dissent and Democracy: Civil Society and the State in Ireland.* Dublin: A&A Farmar.

Ó Broin, Deiric and Andrew Moore. 2011. 'Dublin 5th Province – Citizen Interaction in an e-Deliberation Environment', paper presented at *Beyond the Ballot: Forms of Citizen Engagement between Democratic Elections* - Deliberative and Participatory Democracy Panel for PSAI Annual Conference 2011, UCD, Newman House, Dublin 2 on October 21st 2011.

Ó Broin, Deiric and Eugene Watters. 2007. *Governing Below the Centre: Local Governance in Ireland.* Dublin: New Island.

O'Donnell, Rory and Damian Thomas, 1998. 'Partnership and policy making', in Seán Healy and Brigid Reynolds (eds) *Social Policy in Ireland: Principles, Practice and Problems.* Dublin: Oak Tree Press.

O'Donnell, Rory and Colm O'Reardon. 2000. 'Social Partnership in Ireland's Economic Transformation', in Giuseppe Fajertag and Philippe Pochet (eds) *Social Pacts in Europe—New Dynamics.* Brussels: European Trade Union Institute/Observatoire Social Europeen.

P

Paasche, Silke. 2010. 'Improving the Democratic Quality of EU Policy Making: What Role for the Participation of People Experiencing Homelessness?', in *European Journal of Homelessness,* Volume 4: 249-259.

Papadopoulos, Yannis. 2003. 'Cooperative forms of governance: Problems of democratic accountability in complex environments', in *European Journal of Political Research,* Volume 42 (4): 473-502.

Perkins, Rachel, Gráinne Moran, Jude Cosgrove and Gerry Shiel. 2010. *PISA 2009: The Performance and Progress of 15-year-olds in Ireland.* Dublin: Educational Research Centre.

Pestoff, Victor. 2009.'Towards a Paradigm of Democratic Participation: Citizen Participation and Co-production of Personal Social Services in Sweden', in *Annals of Public and Cooperative Economics*, Volume 80 (2): 197–224.

Pettit, Phillip. 1999. *Republicanism: A Theory of Freedom and Government*. Oxford: Oxford University Press.

Phillips, Anne. 2004. 'Democracy, Recognition and Power', in Frederik Engelstad, Oyvind Osterud and Yevind Sterud (eds) *Power and Democracy, Critical Interventions*. Aldershot: Ashgate.

Piven, Frances Fox. 2008. 'Can Power From Below Change the World', in *American Sociological Review*, Volume 73 (1): 1-14

Piven, Frances Fox, and Richard A. Cloward. 1991. 'Collective Protest: A Critique of Resource Mobilization Theory', in *International Journal of Politics, Culture, and Society*, Volume 4 (4): 435-458.

Powell, Fred. 2007. *The Politics of Civil Society: Neoliberalism or Social Left*. Bristol: Policy Press.

Putnam, Robert. 1993. *Making Democracy Work: Civic Traditions in Modern Italy*. Princeton: Princeton University Press.

R

Richardson, Ann. 1983. *Participation*. London: Routledge & Kegan Paul.

Roche, William K. 1994. 'Pay Determination and the Politics of Industrial Relations,' in Thomas V. Murphy and William K. Roche (eds) *Irish Industrial Relations in Practice*. Dublin: Oak Tree Press.

Roco, Mihail C. 2003. 'Broader societal issues of nanotechnology', in *Journal of Nanoparticle Research*, Volume 5 (3-4): 181–189.

Roco, Mihail C. and William Sims Bainbridge WS (eds). 2001. *Societal Implications of Nanoscience and Nanotechnology (NSET Workshop Report)*. Virginia: National Science Foundation.

Royall, Frédéric. 2002. 'Building Solidarity Across National Boundaries: The Case of Affiliates of the European Network of the Unemployed', in *Journal of European Area Studies*, Volume 10 (2): 243-258.

Royal Society and the Royal Academy of Engineering. 2004. *Nanoscience and nanotechnologies: opportunities and uncertainties*, available at: http://www.nanotec.org.uk/finalReport.htm , last accessed November 18th 2012.

Ruddock, Alan. 2006. "Rotten Social Partnership Deal Eroding Democracy" in *The Sunday Independent, 18th* June 2006.

Russell, Cormac. 2006. *Community Development in Ireland: A Fresh Perspective*. Dublin: Nurture Development Limited.

S

Sandel, Michael. 1996. *Democracy's Discontent: America in Search of a Public Philosophy*. Cambridge: Harvard University Press.

Sandman, Peter, and Jody Lanard. 2005. 'Bird Flu: Communicating the Risk', in *Perspectives on Health*, Volume 10 (2): 2-9.

Science Foundation Ireland. 2010. *Science Foundation Ireland: Celebrating 10 years of Discovery*. Dublin: Government Publications.

Schot, Johan and Arie Rip. 1997. 'The Past and Future of Constructive Technology Assessment', in *Technological Forecasting and Social Change*, Volume 54 (2-3): 251–268.

Schumpeter, Joseph. 1976 [1942]. *Capitalism, Socialism and Democracy*. London: Allen and Unwin.

Scott, Allen J. 2006. *Geography and Economy (Clarendon Lectures in Geography and Environmental Studies)*. Oxford: Oxford University Press.

Scott, Allen J. and Michael Storper. 2003. Regions, Globalization, Development', in *Regional Studies*, Volume 37 (6-7): 579-593.

Scottish Executive. 2005. *National Standards for Community Engagement*. Edinburgh: Communities Scotland.

Shakespeare, Tom. 1993. 'Disabled People's Self-Organisation: A New Social Movement?', in *Disability Handicap and Society*, Volume 8 (3): 249-264.

Shapin, Steven and Simon Schaffer. 1989. *Leviathan and the Air-pump: Hobbes, Boyle, and the Experimental Life*. Princeton: Princeton University Press.

Singh, Jasber. 2005. 'Polluted waters: The UK Nanojury as upstream public engagement', available at: http://www.nanojury.org.uk/pdfs/polluted_waters. pdf, last accessed November 18th 2012.

Smith, Anna Maria. 1998. *Laclau and Mouffe: The Radical Democratic Imaginary*. London: Routledge.

Smith, Graham. 2005. *Beyond The Ballot: 57 Democratic Innovations From Around The World*. London: The Power Inquiry.

Stafford, Peter. 2011. 'The rise and fall of social partnership: its impact on interest group lobbying in Ireland', in *Journal of Public Affairs*, Volume 11 (2): 74-79.

Stoker, Gerry. 2012 . 'Economic Recovery and the Politics of the Long-Term', paper presented at the SPERI Inaugural Conference: Sheffield University, *The British Growth Crisis: The Search for a New Model*, July 16-18, 2012.

Swinnen, Hugo. 2007. *Peer Review and Assessment in Social Inclusion, The NAPinclusion Social Inclusion Forum – Synthesis Report*. Brussels: European Commission.

T

Tierney, John. 2006. 'The Importance of the Local in a Global Context', in David Jacobson, Peadar Kirby and Deiric Ó Broin (eds) *Taming the Tiger: Social Exclusion in a Globalised Ireland*. Dublin: New Island Press.

Toumey, Chris 2011. 'Democratizing nanotech, then and now', in *Nature Nanotechnology*, Volume 6: 605–606.

Trench, Brian. 2003. 'Science, Culture and Public Affairs', in *The Republic,* Volume 3: 53-63.

Trench, Brian. 2009. 'Representations of the Knowledge Economy - Irish Newspapers' Discourses on a Key Policy Idea', in *Irish Communications Review,* Volume 11: 3-20.

U

Unger, Roberto. 2011. *We go to Sleep and We Drown Our Sorrows in Consumption.* Interview with Cora Currier, The European Oct 24th 2011, available at: http://theeuropean-magazine.com/385-unger-roberto/386-the-future-of-the-left, last accessed November 18th 2012.

W

Wagner, David and Marcia B. Cohen. 1991. The Power of the People: Homeless Protesters in the Aftermath of Social Movement Participation', in *Social Problems,* Volume 38 (4): 543-561.

Weinz, Wolfgang. 1986. 'Economic development and interest groups,' in Brian Girvin and Roland Sturm (eds) *Politics and Society in Contemporary Ireland.* Aldershot: Gower.

Williams, Jean Calterone. 2005. 'The Politics of Homelessness: Shelter Now and Political Protest', in *Political Research Quarterly,* Volume 58 (3): 497-507.

Wright, Erik Olin. 2012a. 'Transforming Capitalism through Real Utopias', in American Sociological Review, Volume XX (X): 1-25.

Wright, Erik Olin. 2012b. *'Alternatives within and beyond capitalism: towards a social socialism',* available at http://newdeals.ie/data/documents/ Alternatives_within_and_beyond_capitalism_Nicos_Poulantzas_Institute_lectu re_-_with_figures_at_the_end-2.pdf, last December 1st 2012.

Wynne, Brian. 2005. 'Risk as globalising 'democratic' discourse? Framing subjects and citizens', in Melissa Leach, Ian Scoones and Brian Wynne (eds) *Science and Citizens: Globalisation and the Challenge of Engagement.* London and New York: Zed Books.

INDEX

Lightning Source UK Ltd.
Milton Keynes UK
UKOW040613240413

209643UK00001BA/8/P